ANTI-SEMITE
AND JEW

50 years of publishing
1945-1995

ANTI-SEMITE AND JEW

JEAN-PAUL SARTRE

TRANSLATED BY George J. Becker
PREFACE BY Michael Walzer

Schocken Books   New York

Copyright 1948 by Schocken Books Inc.
Copyright renewed 1976 by Schocken Books Inc.

Preface copyright © 1995 by Michael Walzer

All rights reserved under International and Pan-American
Copyright Conventions. Published in the United States by
Schocken Books Inc., New York. Distributed by Pantheon
Books, a division of Random House, Inc., New York.
Originally published in France as *Réflexions sur la
Question Juive*, by Éditions Morihien, Copyright 1946 by
Paul Morihien, Paris.

Library of Congress Cataloging-in-Publication Data

Sartre, Jean Paul, 1905–
   [Réflexions sur la question juive. English]
   Anti-Semite and Jew / Jean-Paul Sartre ; translated by George J.
 Becker ; with a new preface by Michael Walzer.
       p.   cm.
   Previously published: New York : Schocken Books, 1948.
   ISBN 0-8052-1047-4
   1. Antisemitism.   I. Title.
 DS145.S2713   1995
 305.892'4—dc20   95-1929
                        CIP

Manufactured in the United States of America
First Schocken paperback edition published in 1965

PREFACE

Sometime in the second half of 1944, as the war in Europe drew to a close, Jean-Paul Sartre noticed that in discussions about postwar France, the imminent return of French Jews deported by the Nazis was never mentioned. Some of the speakers, he guessed, were not pleased by the prospect; others, friends of the Jews, thought it best to be silent. (Neither they nor Sartre knew how many of the deported Jews would never return.) Thinking about these discussions, Sartre decided to write a critique of anti-Semitism. Both the occasion and the subject of the critique were French. Having lived through the occupation, writing a year or so before the great celebration of the resistance began, Sartre addressed the complicity of the French in the Nazi project. He did so, however, at a level of abstraction that only few of the French found disturbing. The critique, as it turned out, was more disturbing to the

Jews, with whom Sartre meant to declare his solidarity.

Sartre provides no account of the writing of *Anti-Semite and Jew*. The book must have been composed at breakneck speed, for it was ready to be excerpted in one of the first issues of *Temps Modernes*, founded in 1945. Though Sartre reports on a number of conversations with friends and acquaintances, he says that he did no research. He had read, of course, the most influential anti-Semitic writers—Charles Maurras and Maurice Barrès; and he had encountered anti-Semitism in his own family and among schoolmates at the Lycée. But he did not stop now to read about Jewish history or religion, and the only Jews that he knew were highly assimilated, with little more understanding than he had of either one. Among committed Jews he had no connections of any kind. So he wrote what he thought, describing a world that he knew only in part, reconstructing it in conformity with existentialist psychology and enlightenment skepticism and the version of Marxist class analysis that he had made his own. (In the 1940s, he regularly denied that he was a Marxist, but his commitment-to-come is evident in this book.) He produced a philosophical speculation variously supported by anecdotes and personal observations.

The result, however, is a powerfully coherent argument that demonstrates how theoretical sophistication and practical ignorance can, sometimes, usefully combine.

There is much to criticize in the essay: reading it again fifty years after it was written, one sees immediately how much it was shaped by a specific (and no longer entirely persuasive) political orientation. Its ignorance of Judaism was willful and programmatic—for this parochial religious doctrine, and the community it shaped, and all such doctrines and communities, had no place in the world to come as Sartre conceived it, after the liberation of France and the future liberation of humankind. But the world as it is, France in 1944, is also Sartre's subject. He saw clearly that the defeat of the Nazis was not yet the end of the European catastrophe, and he set out, like many other intellectuals in the 1940s and '50s, to understand the rootedness of prejudice, hatred, and genocide in his own society. *Anti-Semite and Jew*, in its best passages, stands with Theodor Adorno's study of the authoritarian personality, Talcott Parsons' essays on the sociology of Nazism, Erich Fromm's *Escape from Freedom*, and Hannah Arendt's account of totalitarian politics.

But Sartre's book should not be read as a piece of social science or even (as I have described it) as a philosophical speculation. His best work in the 1940s was in drama (*No Exit* was first performed in 1944; *The Respectful Prostitute* in 1946; *Dirty Hands* in 1948), and *Anti-Semite and Jew* is a Marxist/existentialist morality play,

whose characters are produced by their dramatic interactions. The interactions are never actually enacted by
people with proper names; the dialogue is never rendered
in the first person. Everything remains abstract, impersonal, and yet the "situations" and the "choices" are
highly dramatic. As in *No Exit*, the cast of characters is
small. It consists of four actors: the anti-Semite, the
democrat, the inauthentic Jew, the authentic Jew. The
first and third of these play the leads; the second and
fourth have only minor parts—hence the drama is grim,
not tragic finally, but savagely critical of the world it
describes. Waiting offstage to redeem the criticism is the
revolutionary worker.

This is the structure of the Sartrean drama: each character creates the others and chooses himself—and does
both from the inside of a "situation" that Sartre commonly describes in a manner, at least partly learned from
Marx, that suggests its determinist character. The drama
arises from the interplay of social forces and individual
decisions. It is virtually impossible to judge the relative
weight of these two. While Sartre always insists that individuals are responsible not only for what they do but also
for what they are, it is nonetheless clear that they make
their choices under duress.

The tension is most apparent in the portrait of the anti-
Semite, which is commonly and rightly taken to be the

strongest part of the book. The anti-Semite is first of all a social-psychological type, shaped by the narrowness and vulnerability of the world he inhabits (Sartre writes about all four of his characters as if they were men, so I will use masculine pronouns in discussing them). The description is familiar today, though Sartre is one of the first writers to provide it. The anti-Semite comes from the lower middle class of the provincial towns: he is a functionary, office worker, small businessman—a "white collar proletarian." Member of a declining social class, he is threatened by social change, endlessly fearful and resentful. He "possesses nothing," but by identifying the Jew as an alien, he lays claim to all of France. He is moved by a "nostalgia for . . . the primitive community" in which he can claim ascriptive membership: French by birth, language, and history, here he doesn't need to prove either his identity or his worth. The diversity and complexity of "modern social organization" are beyond his understanding; social mobility frightens him; the modern forms of property (abstractions like money and securities) are wholly mysterious to him. He sees the Jew as the initiate in these mysteries, the representative of modernity, the enemy of real Frenchmen, real property, the land, tradition, social order, sentimental attachment—capitalist, communist, atheist, traitor. And he aims, finally, to destroy this sinister threat: "What [the anti-Semite] wishes, what he prepares, is the *death* of the Jew."

The rich, Sartre says, exploit anti-Semitism "rather than abandon themselves to it." And among workers, he confidently claims, "we find scarcely any anti-Semitism." This very precise class analysis, which locates the anti-Semite in a fairly narrow segment of French society, poses a problem for Sartre's argument: if only a part of the society is anti-Semitic, why is the situation of the Jew so radically determined by anti-Semitism? In fact, Sartre is not wholly committed to his class analysis. He starts indeed, from his own circle of family and friends, who came, mostly, out of the provincial petty bourgeoisie, but he moves on to a more abstract characterization. Anti-Semitism is also "a free and total choice of oneself," and this choice, it seems, is made at every level of French society. Sartre gives his readers a sense of pervasive anti-Semitism, motivated by a general fear, not only of specifically modern uncertainties but also of "the human condition," which is to say, of liberty, responsibility, solitude, and truth ("that thing of indefinite approximation"—Sartre's argument about the fear of truth is very much like Adorno's "intolerance of ambiguity"). Some people, the lower middle class especially, are more threatened than others, but no one is entirely unafraid or incapable of choosing the Jew as his enemy and himself as an anti-Semite.

The anti-Semite creates the Jew, but before that he creates himself within his situation. (But isn't this situation in part the creation of the Jew as the anti-Semite has created him? Sartre's argument is necessarily circular. The inauthentic Jew, who appears later on in the drama, is in fact an agent—though not the only or the most important agent—of the modernity to which anti-Semites react.) Sartre sometimes writes as if anti-Semitism is a sociological reflex, but it is also, again, a choice. Indeed, it is the very model of an inauthentic choice, for the anti-Semite cannot or will not acknowledge his actual class situation or the fear it produces. He responds willfully to a world that he willfully misrepresents. Though Sartre never quite says this, it is strictly in line with his argument: anti-Semitism is the inauthenticity of the lower middle class (and of any one else who adopts it). But he never suggests what authentic lower middle class men or women would look like or how they would act—perhaps he doubted that authenticity was a likely, even if it was a possible, choice for members of a declining social class.

Authenticity is clearly not represented by the democrat, another bourgeois figure and the second of Sartre's *dramatis personae*. The democrat embodies the virtues of the French revolution. A good liberal, political centrist, defender of decency, friend—so he would certainly claim—of the Jews, he believes in the universal rights of man, and he wants those rights to be recognized and exercised *right now*. But his is a false universalism for he is blind to the realities of the world he actually inhabits. He cannot acknowledge the strength of anti-Semitism or the concrete conditions of Jewish life, and so he fears and rejects any authentic Jewish response. In an exactly similar fashion, he cannot acknowledge the actual condition of the working class, and so he fears and rejects authentic class consciousness.

The democrat defends the Jew as a man but "annihilates him as a Jew" (compare the argument of Clermont-Tonnerre in the Constituent Assembly's 1791 debate on Jewish citizenship: "One must refuse everything to the Jews as a nation, and give everything to the Jews as individuals. . . ."). But it is as a Jew (and a member of the Jewish nation) that the Jew is perceived by the others, and this is an identity that he cannot escape—more accurately, that he is not allowed to escape. So the democrat's advocacy of assimilation for the Jews and classlessness for the workers, though no doubt well-intentioned, is also cruelly premature. And timing is crucial for Sartre; his drama is historical as well as sociological; it moves in stages. The anti-Semite lives fearfully in the past; the democrat lives naively, sentimentally, inauthentically in the future.

By contrast, the inauthentic Jew lives in what is for him a desperate present. He seeks "avenues of escape," but the more he flees, the more he is trapped: the quintessential modern man. Exactly what is he fleeing from? Sartre's answer to this question is the most problematic part of his argument—first, because it is far less clear than the smooth surface of his essay suggests; and second, because its most insistent claims are radically implausible. Sartre starts with an absence: Jewishness in the modern world, he announces, is an empty category. As a result of "twenty-five centuries" of dispersion, dissolution, and political impotence (Sartre dates the Jewish collapse from the Babylonian exile, not the destruction of the Temple), the Jews are an ancient but also an "unhistorical people." This last term, borrowed from Hegel and Marx, suggests a political/cultural backwater, cut off from all progressive currents. Contemporary Jews have, on this view, no civilization of their own; they cannot take pride in any specifically Jewish collective achievements; they have nothing to remember but a "long martyrdom [and] a long passivity." More than any other minority group, then, they are "perfectly assimilable" into the surrounding culture. Only anti-Semitism, with its construction of the Jew as alien, unpatriotic, cosmopolitan, bars the way.

But then one would expect the inauthentic or escapist Jew to do everything he can to deny the construction and to make himself, in France, more French than the French. He should hide, pass, intermarry, convert, buy land, move to the provinces, adopt conservative or at least conventional political views. Indeed, there have always been Jews who acted in this way, more or less successfully. Other Jews have named them with some functional equivalent of inauthenticity—more obviously morally laden, which Sartre insists his own term is not: unfaithful, false, disloyal. But Sartre's inauthentic Jews are driven in the opposite direction; they are evermore critical, cosmopolitan, ironic, rationalist, and so on. No doubt, this is a portrait (and in its psychosocial detail often a shrewd and insightful portrait) of the assimilated Jewish intellectuals whom Sartre knew in the 1930s and '40s, many of them refugees from the East. But these people were not only trying to escape anti-Semitism and the anti-Semite's construction of Jewishness, they were also escaping the closed communities and orthodox traditionalism of their own Jewish past—a presence, not an absence. Sartre's analysis requires an account of this substantive Judaism, for without it he cannot explain why the Jew in flight conforms so closely to the conception he is supposedly fleeing.

If he were to provide this account, he would also be able to acknowledge that the "avenues of escape" described in his book are chosen in part because of an elective affinity between classical Jewish learning and modernist intellectualism. I don't mean to suggest an identity here, only an affinity—and one that is more a matter of style than of content. The content of Jewish learning is often, obviously, anti-modernist. Nonetheless, one can recognize the interpretative freedom, the pursuit of complexity for its own sake, and the argumentative zeal of the classical yeshiva in the literary and political work of Sartre's Jewish contemporaries. No doubt, the cosmopolitan and leftist politics of (many) of these people served their interests vis-à-vis both Jewish orthodoxy and French anti-Semitism. Many communist Jews, to take the easiest example, were hiding from their Jewishness in the Party, while seeking a world—to which Sartre also aspired, presumably for different reasons—in which Jewishness would not matter. Nonetheless, Jewish leftism was not simply an invention of inauthentic Jews; its cast of mind, intellectual tenor, and modes of analysis resonated clearly with an older culture whose very existence Sartre denies.

Most of the features of Jewish intellectual success in

the modern world are attributed by Sartre to the flight from anti-Semitic constructions of Jewishness. Self-analysis, reflectiveness, skepticism, irony, rationalism, objectivity, abstraction, the "critical turn"—aren't these the marks of the greatest Jewish figures of the modern age: Spinoza, Marx, Freud, Kafka, Proust, Einstein? But aren't these also the very figures that the anti-Semite invokes in order to prove that the Jews are endlessly subversive, acid eating away at the social fabric, corroding all traditional values? Even as they flee their Jewishness, supposedly an anti-Semitic creation, they act out their designated role and confirm the anti-Semite in his fear and hatred. Perhaps the avenue of escape is not well chosen. Or perhaps Jewish modernism isn't merely reactive—so that our understanding of it requires also a deeper understanding of the Jewish past.

Even the authentic Jew, however, has no such understanding. He, too, as Sartre describes him, is a creature of the present. He affirms his Jewish identity, but this affirmation has nothing to do with religious faith, or nostalgia for the old community, or a search for value in the tradition. It is simply an acceptance of the "situation" that the anti-Semite has created and a spirited defense of the physical life of the Jews within it (remember that they have, according to Sartre, no cultural life). Political Zionism is one example of this defense; the American

Anti-Defamation League would be another; Sartre praises a "Jewish league against anti-Semitism" then in formation in France. Just as authentic workers—his constant analogy—reject the myth of social harmony, recognize the reality of class conflict, and make themselves into militant defenders of working class interests, so authentic Jews give up the universalist false consciousness of the democrat, recognize social pluralism, and make themselves into militant defenders of Jewish interests. But there is no real equivalence here. Jewish authenticity is only a way of living well within the Jewish situation; it has no transformative force. (Years later, when he visited Israel in 1967, Sartre revised this judgement: Zionism had created a "new Israeli Jew [who], if he can develop in peace and understand all his contradictions and go beyond them in his actions . . . will be one of the most superior men to be found in history." Neither in 1944 nor in 1967 did Sartre display any gift for understatement.) That is why the authentic Jew is only a minor character in the Sartrean drama. But the authentic worker is a revolutionary and, therefore, a key figure in what we might think of as the next play. Sadly, the anti-Semite and the inauthentic Jew are the key figures in this play, each of them creating and confirming the other's existence, locked together in a world from which there is, until the revolution, no exit.

The working class militant waits in the wings. One day, not quite yet, he will appear dramatically in history, creating a classless society, which represents for Sartre the end of every form of social division. The Jews will assimilate into this society, leaving nothing behind, without regret, giving up their Jewishness just as the worker gives up class consciousness for the sake of universality. Exactly what happens to the lower middle class provincial anti-Semite in the course of the revolution is unclear. Defeated, he presumably disappears from the Sartrean stage, along with the Jew he created.

But this is an ending to be wished for only on the (false) assumption that there really is no Jewish history, culture, or community. Nor are the Jews the only people about whom this assumption would have to be made. The anti-Semite "chooses" the Jew only because he is available; any dispossessed, stigmatized minority, any "unhistorical people" could as easily be chosen. The Jew in Europe is the exposed face of modern life. But the same role can be played, with the same degree of authenticity and inauthenticity, by other groups in other times and places. None of these groups have, in Sartre's eyes, any claim on our moral attention beyond the claim they make as persecuted men and women. We should defend the group's existence only so long as its members are persecuted *as a group*; after that, we defend only their individual rights. Sartre calls this position, which is his own, "concrete liberalism." Indeed, he is a liberal, for all his Marxizing sociology.

But he is not a pluralist liberal. The disappearance of historical peoples, like the French, is obviously not on his agenda, and so he must imagine a future international society of distinct nations (he would, of course, and in the years to come he did, oppose every version of imperial and chauvinist politics, including the French version). With regard to a future France, however, he adopts a radically antipluralist position. This position is always described in social and economic rather than cultural terms: Sartre looks forward to a France "whose members feel mutual bonds of solidarity, because they are all engaged in the same enterprise." But he doesn't want to repeat the error of the democrat: solidarity and mutual engagement do not exist and cannot exist in contemporary France, where class conflict creates and intensifies cultural difference. Here and now, difference must be accepted; there is no honest alternative. So the Jew has to be granted his double identity, welcomed as a "French Jew . . . with his character, his customs, his tastes, his religion if he has one." *Multi-culturalism now*: so we might describe the Sartrean program. But this is, for him, only a temporary and second-best solution to the problem of anti-Semitism. In no sense does it represent a recognition that there might be any value in Jewish character, customs, tastes, or religion.

This historically divided politics—difference now, unity later—is, Sartre believes, what authenticity requires. Even if anti-Semitism "is a mythical . . . representation of the class struggle," it is nonetheless a genuine affliction for the Jews. It reflects the reality of a divided society, "the conflict of interests and the crosscurrents of passions . . . *it is a phenomenon of social pluralism* (emphasis added)." Living authentically within this situation means acknowledging the conflict and then fighting for the rights of oppressed and marginalized groups. This is the point of Sartre's book, which he probably thought of, whatever else he thought of it, as a political manifesto. But his longterm goal is a society where groups no longer exist to be oppressed and marginalized. Once again, Sartre assumes that this is what their members also want. Jewish authenticity is second-best even for the Jew, who longs to be what Sartre already is, French without qualification or addition.

But why is this such an attractive goal? It is attractive to Sartre because of his conviction that social pluralism necessarily leads to conflict, and conflict necessarily produces hatred and oppression. The mythic representation of the "other," the projection of resentment and fear onto some helpless minority—these are for Sartre inevitable consequences of pluralism. He is prepared to fight these consequences, but he is sure that the fight will never be won until pluralism, indeed, groupness itself, is definitively transcended. The revolution will bring a new solidarity, which will have no specific historical or cultural character, the ethnic or national or religious equivalent of classlessness.

This is little more than the conventional left doctrine of Sartre's own time—and before and after, too. Obviously, the strength of *Anti-Semite and Jew* does not lie here; it is the portraits of the main characters that carry the book. Still, it seems worthwhile to suggest an alternative to Sartre's revolutionary transcendence, for his position is likely to look, today, as mythical as the anti-Semite's Jew—and as inauthentic. After all, what would men and women be like after the end of social pluralism? Perhaps Sartre believes that they will be simply and universally human. In fact, as the whole argument of his book suggests, they will surely be French. And this will represent a universal identity only in the sense that it will be universally available to the Jews and to all other non-French minorities. In every other sense, it will be a historically particular identity, culturally rich, no doubt, but not obviously richer or better than the identities it supercedes. Sartre's conviction that minorities like the Jews were eager to assimilate (in his very strong sense of this word) has turned out to be wrong; indeed, it was wrong at the time, in 1944, even if many individuals recognized themselves in his descriptions. *Anti-Semite and Jew* provoked an angrily defensive response from committed Jewish intellectuals, despite Sartre's sympathy not only for their cause but for them, as authentic Jews. They could not accept his insistence that they were, should be, and could only be, heroic defenders of an empty Jewishness.

Even intellectuals heavily influenced by Sartre, like Albert Memmi, who wrote several books analyzing the "concrete negativity" of Jewish life in the diaspora, could not themselves enact a Sartrean authenticity: "To affirm my Jewishness without giving it a specific content," Memmi argued, "would have been an empty proposition and in the final analysis contradictory" (*The Liberation of the Jew*, 1966). And where could that content come from except from "a cultural and religious tradition . . . collective habits of thought and behavior"? Memmi's engagement with the tradition and the habits was in large part oppositional, but it still represented a denial of Sartre's argument about Jewish absence.

Nor could these Jewish intellectuals agree that their role was historically circumscribed and of only temporary use. Memmi was a Zionist, arguing that even after the revolution Jews would need a place of their own: Jewish authenticity—self-affirmation and self-determination

xxii

—was possible only in a Jewish state. Other writers, determined to find a place in France as well as in Israel, argued for a pluralist society—the source, Sartre thought, of all their troubles. They envisaged a *permanent* multiculturalism, an idea that was fully articulated only in the much more radically pluralist United States, where the co-existence of cultural (most importantly religious) difference and common citizenship was figuratively represented by the "hyphenated" American. Characteristically, Sartre, who visited the United States in 1945 and wrote *The Respectful Prostitute* immediately after, saw in American pluralism only oppression and hatred: racism was the anti-Semitism of the new world. He was not entirely wrong, not then, not now. The (relative) success of religious toleration in breaking the link between pluralism and conflict has not yet been repeated for race and ethnicity. But there seems no good reason not to try to repeat it, given the value that people attach to their identity and culture.

Much can be learned, nonetheless, from Sartre's Marxist/existentialist psychology. Identity and culture are not timeless essences; they develop and change within historical situations; and the self-perception of individuals and groups is radically influenced by the (often hostile) perceptions of the "others." All this is true. Sartre is very good at alerting us to the interpersonal construction of personal identities—a process even more in evidence today than when he wrote. At the same time, however, this constructive activity draws on and reinforces the different historical cultures. These have an inner strength that Sartre never acknowledges, and the people they sustain, who also sustain them, are not yet candidates for disappearance.

Nor, indeed, has anti-Semitism disappeared. If its new forms are not accessible to Sartre's particular version of class analysis, they nonetheless require an analysis along roughly similar lines: a search for people in trouble, incapable of understanding or coping with the actual sources of their difficulties, looking for someone to blame. Sometimes these people inhabit the lower middle class milieu that Sartre evoked, but they are also (in contemporary Eastern Europe, for example) workers and peasants and (in the United States) members of the new underclass.

Jews are more likely today than they were in 1944 to respond "authentically" to their encounter with anti-Semitism—that is, to affirm the value of their history and culture. But one contemporary response provides an interesting example of what many Jews today would call inauthenticity, though it is not clear that Sartre would recognize it as such: that is, the effort to base Jewish identity on the Holocaust experience. This is purely reactive to the most terrible work of twentieth century anti-Semites, but the insistence on remembering this work and identifying with its victims hardly represents an "avenue of escape." Sartrean authenticity has taken on new meanings, a sign simultaneously that his argument is persuasive and that it is in need of revision.

Now that the revolution Sartre foresaw has been indefinitely postponed, it is time to imagine a new drama in which the actors live a little more comfortably in each other's eyes . . . and in their own. The aim of a concrete liberalism, one would think, is to design situations from which an honorable escape is possible—but where it is also possible to feel at home, to live with friends and relatives, chosen and inherited, not only in traditional but also in innovative ways, in peace. Rising rates of intermarriage and assimilation, which Sartre predicted would follow naturally from any lifting of anti-Semitic pressure, now stand in tension with developments he neither predicted nor could have understood: the institutional strength of diaspora Jewish communities, the rise of Jewish studies in universities throughout the Western world, the revival of religious interest (if not of religious faith), and a transnational solidarity that extends across the diaspora as well as binding diaspora Jews to Israel.

Sartre's revolutionary transcendence looks today very much like the long-imagined messianic age, around which Jews over the centuries have constructed a set of arguments whose thickness and complexity hardly fit his version of their story. The arguments combine faith, skepticism, worldly wit, and prudence. And at least some of the commentators suggest a position that might fit a chastened Sartreanism: while we wait for the unitary world to come, since the wait is likely to be long, it is urgently necessary and entirely possible to repair and improve the fragmented world, which is the only world we have.*

—Michael Walzer
The Institute for Advanced Study
Princeton, NJ
January 1995

* I am grateful to Menachem Brinker and Mitchell Cohen for their critical reading of an early draft of this preface.

1

If a man attributes all or part of his own misfortunes and those of his country to the presence of Jewish elements in the community, if he proposes to remedy this state of affairs by depriving the Jews of certain of their rights, by keeping them out of certain economic and social activities, by expelling them from the country, by exterminating all of them, we say that he has anti-Semitic *opinions*.

This word *opinion* makes us stop and think. It is the word a hostess uses to bring to an end a discussion that threatens to become acrimonious. It suggests that all points of view are equal; it reassures us, for it gives an inoffensive appearance to ideas by reducing them to the level of tastes. All tastes are natural; all opinions are permitted. Tastes, colors, and opinions are not open to discussion. In the name of democratic institutions, in the name of freedom of opinion, the anti-

Semite asserts the right to preach the anti-Jewish crusade everywhere.

At the same time, accustomed as we have been since the Revolution to look at every object in an analytic spirit, that is to say, as a composite whose elements can be separated, we look upon persons and characters as mosaics in which each stone coexists with the others without that coexistence affecting the nature of the whole. Thus anti-Semitic opinion appears to us to be a molecule that can enter into combination with other molecules of any origin whatsoever without undergoing any alteration. A man may be a good father and a good husband, a conscientious citizen, highly cultivated, philanthropic, *and* in addition an anti-Semite. He may like fishing and the pleasures of love, may be tolerant in matters of religion, full of generous notions on the condition of the natives in Central Africa, *and* in addition detest the Jews. If he does not like them, we say, it is because his experience has shown him that they are bad, because statistics have taught him that they are dangerous, because certain historical factors have influenced his judgment. Thus this opinion seems to be the result of external causes, and those who wish to study it are prone to neglect the personality of the anti-Semite in favor of a consideration of the percentage of Jews who were mobilized in 1914, the percentage of

Jews who are bankers, industrialists, doctors, and lawyers, or an examination of the history of the Jews in France since early times. They succeed in revealing a strictly objective situation that determines an equally objective current of opinion, and this they call anti-Semitism, for which they can draw up charts and determine the variations from 1870 to 1944. In such wise anti-Semitism appears to be at once a subjective taste that enters into combination with other tastes to form a personality, and an impersonal and social phenomenon which can be expressed by figures and averages, one which is conditioned by economic, historical, and political constants.

I do not say that these two conceptions are necessarily contradictory. I do say that they are dangerous and false. I would admit, if necessary, that one may have an opinion on the government's policy in regard to the wine industry, that is, that one may decide, *for certain reasons*, either to approve or condemn the free importation of wine from Algeria: here we have a case of holding an opinion on the administration of things. But I refuse to characterize as opinion a doctrine that is aimed directly at particular persons and that seeks to suppress their rights or to exterminate them. The Jew whom the anti-Semite wishes to lay hands upon is not a schematic being defined solely by his function,

9

as under administrative law; or by his status or his acts, as under the Code. He is a Jew, the son of Jews, recognizable by his physique, by the color of his hair, by his clothing perhaps, and, so they say, by his character. Anti-Semitism does not fall within the category of ideas protected by the right of free opinion.

Indeed, it is something quite other than an idea. It is first of all a *passion*. No doubt it can be set forth in the form of a theoretical proposition. The "moderate" anti-Semite is a courteous man who will tell you quietly: "Personally, I do not detest the Jews. I simply find it preferable, for various reasons, that they should play a lesser part in the activity of the nation." But a moment later, if you have gained his confidence, he will add with more abandon: "You see, there must be *something* about the Jews; they upset me physically."

This argument, which I have heard a hundred times, is worth examining. First of all, it derives from the logic of passion. For, really now, can we imagine anyone's saying seriously: "There must be something about tomatoes, for I have a horror of eating them"? In addition, it shows us that anti-Semitism in its most temperate and most evolved forms remains a syncretic whole which may be expressed by statements of reasonable tenor, but which can involve even bodily modifications. Some men are suddenly struck with impotence if they learn from the woman with whom they are making love that she is a Jewess. There is a disgust for the Jew, just as there is a disgust for the Chinese or the Negro among certain people. Thus it is not from the body that the sense of repulsion arises, since one may love a Jewess very well if one does not know what her race is; rather it is something that enters the body from the mind. It is an involvement of the mind, but one so deep-seated and complete that it extends to the physiological realm, as happens in cases of hysteria.

This involvement is not caused by experience. I have questioned a hundred people on the reasons for their anti-Semitism. Most of them have confined themselves to enumerating the defects with which tradition has endowed the Jews. "I detest them because they are selfish, intriguing, persistent, oily, tactless, etc."—"But, at any rate, you associate with some of them?"—"Not if I can help it!" A painter said to me: "I am hostile to the Jews because, with their critical habits, they encourage our servants to insubordination." Here are examples a little more precise. A young actor without talent insisted that the Jews had kept him from a successful career in the theater by confining him to subordinate roles. A young woman said to me: "I have had the most horrible experiences with furriers; they robbed me, they burned the fur I entrusted to them.

Well, they were all Jews." But why did she choose to hate Jews rather than furriers? Why Jews or furriers rather than such and such a Jew or such and such a furrier? Because she had in her a predisposition toward anti-Semitism.

A classmate of mine at the lycée told me that Jews "annoy" him because of the thousands of injustices that "Jew-ridden" social organizations commit in their favor. "A Jew passed his *agrégation* * the year I was failed, and you can't make me believe that that fellow, whose father came from Cracow or Lemberg, understood a poem by Ronsard or an eclogue by Virgil better than I." But he admitted that he disdained the *agrégation* as a mere academic exercise, and that he didn't study for it. Thus, to explain his failure, he made use of two systems of interpretation, like those madmen who, when they are far gone in their madness, pretend to be the King of Hungary but, if questioned sharply, admit to being shoemakers. His thoughts moved on two planes without his being in the least embarrassed by it. As a matter of fact, he will in time manage to justify his past laziness on the grounds that it really would be too stupid to prepare for an examination in which Jews are passed in preference to good Frenchmen. Actually

---

* Competitive state teachers' examination.

12

ne ranked twenty-seventh on the official list. There were twenty-six ahead of him, twelve who passed and fourteen who failed. Suppose Jews had been excluded from the competition; would that have done him any good? And even if he had been at the top of the list of unsuccessful candidates, even if by eliminating one of the successful candidates he would have had a chance to pass, why should the Jew Weil have been eliminated rather than the Norman Mathieu or the Breton Arzell? To understand my classmate's indignation we must recognize that he had adopted in advance a certain idea of the Jew, of his nature and of his role in society. And to be able to decide that among twenty-six competitors who were more successful than himself, it was the Jew who robbed him of his place, he must a priori have given preference in the conduct of his life to reasoning based on passion. Far from experience producing his idea of the Jew, it was the latter which explained his experience. If the Jew did not exist, the anti-Semite would invent him.

That may be so, you will say, but leaving the question of experience to one side, must we not admit that anti-Semitism is explained by certain historical data? For after all it does not come out of the air. It would be easy for me to reply that the history of France tells us nothing about the Jews: they were oppressed right up to 1789; since then they have participated as best they could in the life of the nation, taking advantage, naturally, of freedom of competition to displace the weak, but no more and no less than other Frenchmen. They have committed no crimes against France, have engaged in no treason. And if people believe there is proof that the number of Jewish soldiers in 1914 was lower than it should have been, it is because someone had the curiosity to consult statistics. This is not one of those facts which have the power to strike the imagination by themselves; no soldier in the trenches was able on his own initiative to feel astonishment at not seeing any Jews in the narrow sector that constituted his universe. However, since the information that history gives on the role of Israel depends essentially on the conception one has of history, I think it would be better to borrow from a foreign country a manifest example of "Jewish treason" and to calculate the repercussions this "treason" may have had on contemporary anti-Semitism.

In the course of the bloody Polish revolts of the nineteenth century, the Warsaw Jews, whom the czars handled gently for reasons of policy, were very lukewarm toward the rebels. By not taking part in the insurrection they were able to maintain and improve their position in a country ruined by repression.

I don't know whether this is true or not. What is certain is that many Poles believe it, and this "historical fact" contributes not a little to their bitterness against the Jews. But if I examine the matter more closely, I discover a vicious circle: The czars, we are told, treated the Polish Jews well whereas they willingly ordered pogroms against those in Russia. These sharply different courses of action had the same cause. The Russian government considered the Jews in both Russia and Poland to be unassimilable; according to the needs of their policy, they had them massacred at Moscow and Kiev because they were a danger to the Russian empire, but favored them at Warsaw as a means of stirring up discord among the Poles. The latter showed nothing but hate and scorn for the Jews of Poland, but the reason was the same: For them Israel could never become an integral part of the national collectivity. Treated as Jews by the czar and as Jews by the Poles, provided, quite in spite of themselves, with Jewish interests in the midst of a foreign community, is it any wonder that these members of a minority behaved in accordance with the representation made of them?

In short, the essential thing here is not an "historical fact" but the idea that the agents of history formed for themselves of the Jew. When the Poles of today harbor resentment against the Jews for their past conduct, they are incited to it by that same idea. If one is going to reproach little children for the sins of their grandfathers, one must first of all have a very primitive conception of what constitutes responsibility. Furthermore one must form his conception of the children on the basis of what the grandparents have been. One must believe that what their elders did the young are capable of doing. One must convince himself that Jewish character is inherited. Thus the Poles of 1940 treated the Israelites in the community as *Jews* because their ancestors in 1848 had done the same with their contemporaries. Perhaps this traditional representation would, under other circumstances, have disposed the Jews of today to act like those of 1848. It is therefore the *idea* of the Jew that one forms for himself which would seem to determine history, not the "historical fact" that produces the idea.

People speak to us also of "social facts," but if we look at this more closely we shall find the same vicious circle. There are too many Jewish lawyers, someone says. But is there any complaint that there are too many Norman lawyers? Even if all the Bretons were doctors would we say anything more than that "Brittany provides doctors for the whole of France"? Oh, someone will answer, it is not at all the same thing. No doubt, but that is precisely because we consider Normans as

16

Normans and Jews as Jews. Thus wherever we turn it is the *idea of the Jew* which seems to be the essential thing.

It has become evident that no external factor can induce anti-Semitism in the anti-Semite. Anti-Semitism is a free and total choice of oneself, a comprehensive attitude that one adopts not only toward Jews but toward men in general, toward history and society; it is at one and the same time a passion and a conception of the world. No doubt in the case of a given anti-Semite certain characteristics will be more marked than in another. But they are always all present at the same time, and they influence each other. It is this syncretic totality which we must now attempt to describe.

I noted earlier that anti-Semitism is a passion. Everybody understands that emotions of hate or anger are involved. But ordinarily hate and anger have a *provocation:* I hate someone who has made me suffer, someone who contemns or insults me. We have just seen that anti-Semitic passion could not have such a character. It precedes the facts that are supposed to call it forth; it seeks them out to nourish itself upon them; it must even interpret them in a special way so that they may become truly offensive. Indeed, if you so much as mention a Jew to an anti-Semite, he will show all the signs of a lively irritation. If we recall that we must always *consent* to anger before it can manifest itself and

17

that, as is indicated so accurately by the French idiom, we "put ourselves" into anger, we shall have to agree that the anti-Semite has *chosen* to live on the plane of passion. It is not unusual for people to elect to live a life of passion rather than one of reason. But ordinarily they love the *objects* of passion: women, glory, power, money. Since the anti-Semite has chosen hate, we are forced to conclude that it is the *state* of passion that he loves. Ordinarily this type of emotion is not very pleasant: a man who passionately desires a woman is impassioned because of the woman and in spite of his passion. We are wary of reasoning based on passion, seeking to support by all possible means opinions which love or jealousy or hate have dictated. We are wary of the aberrations of passion and of what is called mono-ideism. But that is just what the anti-Semite chooses right off.

How can one choose to reason falsely? It is because of a longing for impenetrability. The rational man groans as he gropes for the truth; he knows that his reasoning is no more than tentative, that other considerations may supervene to cast doubt on it. He never sees very clearly where he is going; he is "open"; he may even appear to be hesitant. But there are people who are attracted by the durability of a stone. They wish to be massive and impenetrable; they wish not to

18

change. Where, indeed, would change take them? We have here a basic fear of oneself and of truth. What frightens them is not the content of truth, of which they have no conception, but the form itself of truth, that thing of indefinite approximation. It is as if their own existence were in continual suspension. But they wish to exist all at once and right away. They do not want any acquired opinions; they want them to be innate. Since they are afraid of reasoning, they wish to lead the kind of life wherein reasoning and research play only a subordinate role, wherein one seeks only what he has already found, wherein one becomes only what he already was. This is nothing but passion. Only a strong emotional bias can give a lightninglike certainty; it alone can hold reason in leash; it alone can remain impervious to experience and last for a whole lifetime.

The anti-Semite has chosen hate because hate is a faith; at the outset he has chosen to devaluate words and reasons. How entirely at ease he feels as a result. How futile and frivolous discussions about the rights of the Jew appear to him. He has placed himself on other ground from the beginning. If out of courtesy he consents for a moment to defend his point of view, he lends himself but does not give himself. He tries simply to project his intuitive certainty onto the plane of discourse. I mentioned awhile back some remarks by anti-Semites, all of them absurd: "I hate Jews because they make servants insubordinate, because a Jewish furrier robbed me, etc." Never believe that anti-Semites are completely unaware of the absurdity of their replies. They know that their remarks are frivolous, open to challenge. But they are amusing themselves, for it is their adversary who is obliged to use words responsibly, since he believes in words. The anti-Semites have the *right* to play. They even like to play with discourse for, by giving ridiculous reasons, they discredit the seriousness of their interlocutors. They delight in acting in bad faith, since they seek not to persuade by sound argument but to intimidate and disconcert. If you press them too closely, they will abruptly fall silent, loftily indicating by some phrase that the time for argument is past. It is not that they are afraid of being convinced. They fear only to appear ridiculous or to prejudice by their embarrassment their hope of winning over some third person to their side.

If then, as we have been able to observe, the anti-Semite is impervious to reason and to experience, it is not because his conviction is strong. Rather his conviction is strong because he has chosen first of all to be impervious.

He has chosen also to be terrifying. People are afraid

of irritating him. No one knows to what lengths the aberrations of his passion will carry him—but he knows, for this passion is not provoked by something external. He has it well in hand; it is obedient to his will: now he lets go the reins and now he pulls back on them. He is not afraid of himself, but he sees in the eyes of others a disquieting image—his own—and he makes his words and gestures conform to it. Having this external model, he is under no necessity to look for his personality within himself. He has chosen to find his being entirely outside himself, never to look within, to be nothing save the fear he inspires in others. What he flees even more than Reason is his intimate awareness of himself. But someone will object: What if he is like that only with regard to the Jews? What if he otherwise conducts himself with good sense? I reply that that is impossible. There is the case of a fishmonger who, in 1942, annoyed by the competition of two Jewish fishmongers who were concealing their race, one fine day took pen in hand and denounced them. I have been assured that this fishmonger was in other respects a mild and jovial man, the best of sons. But I don't believe it. A man who finds it entirely natural to denounce other men cannot have our conception of humanity; he does not see even those whom he aids in the same light as we do. His generosity, his kindness are not like our kindness, our generosity. You cannot confine passion to one sphere.

The anti-Semite readily admits that the Jew is intelligent and hard-working; he will even confess himself inferior in these respects. This concession costs him nothing, for he has, as it were, put those qualities in parentheses. Or rather they derive their value from the one who possesses them: the more virtues the Jew has the more dangerous he will be. The anti-Semite has no illusions about what he is. He considers himself an average man, modestly average, basically mediocre. There is no example of an anti-Semite's claiming individual superiority over the Jews. But you must not think that he is ashamed of his mediocrity; he takes pleasure in it; I will even assert that he has chosen it. This man fears every kind of solitariness, that of the genius as much as that of the murderer; he is the man of the crowd. However small his stature, he takes every precaution to make it smaller, lest he stand out from the herd and find himself face to face with himself. He has made himself an anti-Semite because that is something one cannot be alone. The phrase, "I hate the Jews," is one that is uttered in chorus; in pronouncing it, one attaches himself to a tradition and to a community—the tradition and community of the mediocre.

We must remember that a man is not necessarily

humble or even modest because he has consented to mediocrity. On the contrary, there is a passionate pride among the mediocre, and anti-Semitism is an attempt to give value to mediocrity as such, to create an elite of the ordinary. To the anti-Semite, intelligence is Jewish; he can thus disdain it in all tranquillity, like all the other virtues which the Jew possesses. They are so many ersatz attributes that the Jew cultivates in place of that balanced mediocrity which he will never have. The true Frenchman, rooted in his province, in his country, borne along by a tradition twenty centuries old, benefiting from ancestral wisdom, guided by tried customs, does not *need* intelligence. His virtue depends upon the assimilation of the qualities which the work of a hundred generations has lent to the objects which surround him; it depends on property. It goes without saying that this is a matter of inherited property, not property one buys. The anti-Semite has a fundamental incomprehension of the various forms of modern property: money, securities, etc. These are abstractions, entities of reason related to the abstract intelligence of the Semite. A security belongs to no one because it can belong to everyone; moreover, it is a sign of wealth, not a concrete possession. The anti-Semite can conceive only of a type of primitive ownership of land based on a veritable magical rapport, in which the thing pos-

23

sessed and its possessor are united by a bond of mystical participation; he is the poet of real property. It transfigures the proprietor and endows him with a special and concrete sensibility. To be sure, this sensibility ignores eternal truths or universal values: the universal is Jewish, since it is an object of intelligence. What his subtle sense seizes upon is precisely that which the intelligence cannot perceive. To put it another way, the principle underlying anti-Semitism is that the concrete possession of a particular object gives as if by magic the meaning of that object. Maurras said the same thing when he declared a Jew to be forever incapable of understanding this line of Racine:

*Dans l'Orient désert, quel devint mon ennui.**

But the way is open to me, mediocre me, to understand what the most subtle, the most cultivated intelligence has been unable to grasp. Why? Because I possess Racine—Racine and my country and my soil. Perhaps the Jew speaks a purer French than I do, perhaps he knows syntax and grammar better, perhaps he is even a writer. No matter; he has spoken this language for only twenty years, and I for a thousand years. The correctness of his style is abstract, acquired; my faults of French are in conformity with the genius of

* *Bérénice.*

the language. We recognize here the reasoning that Barrès used against the holders of scholarships. There is no occasion for surprise. Don't the Jews have all the scholarships? All that intelligence, all that money can acquire one leaves to them, but it is as empty as the wind. The only things that count are irrational values, and it is just these things which are denied the Jews forever. Thus the anti-Semite takes his stand from the start on the ground of irrationalism. He is opposed to the Jew, just as sentiment is to intelligence, the particular to the universal, the past to the present, the concrete to the abstract, the owner of real property to the possessor of negotiable securities.

Besides this, many anti-Semites—the majority, perhaps—belong to the lower middle class of the towns; they are functionaries, office workers, small businessmen, who possess nothing. It is in opposing themselves to the Jew that they suddenly become conscious of being proprietors: in representing the Jew as a robber, they put themselves in the enviable position of people who could be robbed. Since the Jew wishes to take France from them, it follows that France must belong to them. Thus they have chosen anti-Semitism as a means of establishing their status as possessors. The Jew has more money than they? So much the better: money is Jewish, and they can despise it as they despise intelligence. They own less than the gentleman-farmer of Périgord or the large-scale farmer of the Beauce? That doesn't matter. All they have to do is nourish a vengeful anger against the robbers of Israel and they feel at once in possession of the entire country. True Frenchmen, good Frenchmen are all equal, for each of them possesses for himself alone France whole and indivisible.

Thus I would call anti-Semitism a poor man's snobbery. And in fact it would appear that the rich for the most part exploit this passion for their own uses rather than abandon themselves to it—they have better things to do. It is propagated mainly among the middle classes, because they possess neither land nor house nor castle, having only some ready cash and a few securities in the bank. It was not by chance that the petty bourgeoisie of Germany was anti-Semitic in 1925. The principal concern of this "white-collar proletariat" was to distinguish itself from the real proletariat. Ruined by big industry, bamboozled by the Junkers, it was nonetheless to the Junkers and the great industrialists that its whole heart went out. It went in for anti-Semitism with the same enthusiasm that it went in for wearing bourgeois dress: *because* the workers were internationalists, because the Junkers possessed Germany and it wished to possess it also. Anti-Semitism is not merely the joy of hating; it brings positive pleasures too. By treating the Jew as an inferior and pernicious being, I affirm at the same time that I belong to the elite. This elite, in contrast to those of modern times which are based on merit or labor, closely resembles an aristocracy of birth. There is nothing I have to do to merit my superiority, and neither can I lose it. It is given once and for all. It is a *thing*.

We must not confuse this precedence the anti-Semite enjoys by virtue of his principles with individual merit. The anti-Semite is not too anxious to possess individual merit. Merit has to be sought, just like truth; it is discovered with difficulty; one must deserve it. Once acquired, it is perpetually in question: a false step, an error, and it flies away. Without respite, from the beginning of our lives to the end, we are responsible for what merit we enjoy. Now the anti-Semite flees responsibility as he flees his own consciousness, and choosing for his personality the permanence of rock, he chooses for his morality a scale of petrified values. Whatever he does, he knows that he will remain at the top of the ladder; whatever the Jew does, he will never get any higher than the first rung.

We begin to perceive the meaning of the anti-Semite's choice of himself. He chooses the irremediable out of fear of being free; he chooses mediocrity out of fear of being alone, and out of pride he makes of this irremediable mediocrity a rigid aristocracy. To this end he finds the existence of the Jew absolutely necessary. Otherwise to whom would he be superior? Indeed, it is vis-à-vis the Jew and the Jew alone that the anti-Semite realizes that he has rights. If by some miracle all the Jews were exterminated as he wishes, he would find himself nothing but a concierge or a shopkeeper in a strongly hierarchical society in which the quality of "true Frenchman" would be at a low valuation, because everyone would possess it. He would lose his sense of rights over the country because no one would any longer contest them, and that profound equality which brings him close to the nobleman and the man of wealth would disappear all of a sudden, for it is primarily negative. His frustrations, which he has attributed to the disloyal competition of the Jew, would have to be imputed to some other cause, lest he be forced to look within himself. He would run the risk of falling into bitterness, into a melancholy hatred of the privileged classes. Thus the anti-Semite is in the unhappy position of having a vital need for the very enemy he wishes to destroy.

The equalitarianism that the anti-Semite seeks with so much ardor has nothing in common with that equality inscribed in the creed of the democracies. The latter is to be realized in a society that is economically hier-archical, and is to remain compatible with a diversity of functions. But it is in protest *against* the hierarchy of functions that the anti-Semite asserts the equality of Aryans. He does not understand anything about the division of labor and doesn't care about it. From his point of view each citizen can claim the title of French-man, not because he co-operates, in his place or in his occupation, with others in the economic, social, and cultural life of the nation, but because he has, in the same way as everybody else, an imprescriptible and inborn right to the indivisible totality of the country. Thus the society that the anti-Semite conceives of is a society of juxtaposition, as one can very well imagine, since his ideal of property is that of real and basic property. Since, in point of fact, anti-Semites are nu-merous, each of them does his part in constituting a community based on mechanical solidarity in the heart of organized society.

The degree of integration of each anti-Semite with this society, as well as the degree of his equality, is fixed by what I shall call the temperature of the community. Proust has shown, for example, how anti-Semitism brought the duke closer to his coachman, how, thanks to their hatred of Dreyfus, bourgeois families forced the doors of the aristocracy. The equalitarian society

29

that the anti-Semite believes in is like that of mobs or those instantaneous societies which come into being at a lynching or during a scandal. Equality in them is the product of the non-differentiation of functions. The social bond is anger; the collectivity has no other goal than to exercise over certain individuals a diffused repressive sanction. Collective impulsions and stereotypes are imposed on individuals all the more strongly because none of them is defended by any specialized function. Thus the person is drowned in the crowd, and the ways of thinking and reacting of the group are of a purely primitive type. Of course, such collectivities do not spring solely from anti-Semitism; an uprising, a crime, an injustice can cause them to break out suddenly. But those are ephemeral formations which soon vanish without leaving any trace.

Since anti-Semitism survives the great crises of Jew-hatred, the society which the anti-Semites form remains in a latent state during normal periods, with every anti-Semite celebrating its existence. Incapable of understanding modern social organization, he has a nostalgia for periods of crisis in which the primitive community will suddenly reappear and attain its temperature of fusion. He wants his personality to melt suddenly into the group and be carried away by the collective torrent. He has this atmosphere of the pogrom in mind when he asserts "the union of all Frenchmen." In this sense anti-Semitism is, in a democracy, a covert form of what is called the struggle of the citizen against authority. Question any one of those turbulent young men who placidly break the law and band together to beat up a Jew in a deserted street: He will tell you that he wants a strong authority to take from him the crushing responsibility of thinking for himself. Since the Republic is weak, he is led to break the law out of love of obedience. But is it really strong authority that he wishes? In reality he demands rigorous order for others, and for himself disorder without responsibility. He wishes to place himself above the law, at the same time escaping from the consciousness of his liberty and his isolation. He therefore makes use of a subterfuge: The Jews take part in elections; there are Jews in the government; therefore the legal power is vitiated at its base. As a matter of fact, it no longer exists, so it is legitimate to ignore its decrees. Consequently there is no disobedience—one cannot disobey what does not exist. Thus for the anti-Semite there is a *real* France with a government *real* but diffused and without special organs, and an abstract France, official, Jew-ridden, against which it is proper to rebel.

Naturally this permanent rebellion is the act of a group; the anti-Semite would under no circumstances dare to act or think on his own. And the group would be unable to conceive of itself as a minority party, for a minority party is obliged to devise a program and to determine on a line of political action, all of which implies initiative, responsibility, and liberty. Anti-Semitic associations do not wish to invent anything; they refuse to assume responsibility; they would be horrified at setting themselves up as a certain fraction of French opinion, for then they would have to draw up a program and seek legal means of action. They prefer to represent themselves as expressing in all purity, in all passivity, the sentiments of the *real* country in its indivisible state.

Any anti-Semite is therefore, in varying degree, the enemy of constituted authority. He wishes to be the disciplined member of an undisciplined group; he adores order, but a *social* order. We might say that he wishes to provoke political disorder in order to restore social order, the social order in his eyes being a society that, by virtue of juxtaposition, is egalitarian and primitive, one with a heightened temperature, one from which Jews are excluded. These principles enable him to enjoy a strange sort of independence, which I shall call an inverted liberty. Authentic liberty assumes responsibilities, and the liberty of the anti-Semite comes from the fact that he escapes all of his. Floating between an authoritarian society which has not yet come into existence and an official and tolerant society which he disavows, he can do anything he pleases without appearing to be an anarchist, which would horrify him. The profound seriousness of his aims—which no word, no statement, no act can express—permits him a certain frivolity. He is a hooligan, he beats people up, he purges, he robs; it is all in a good cause. If the government is strong, anti-Semitism withers, unless it be a part of the program of the government itself, in which case it changes its nature. Enemy of the Jews, the anti-Semite has need of them. Anti-democratic, he is a natural product of democracies and can only manifest himself within the framework of the Republic.

We begin to understand that anti-Semitism is more than a mere "opinion" about the Jews and that it involves the entire personality of the anti-Semite. But we have not yet finished with him, for he does not confine himself to furnishing moral and political directives: he has a method of thought and a conception of the world all his own. In fact, we cannot state what he affirms without implicit reference to certain intellectual principles.

The Jew, he says, is completely bad, completely a Jew. His virtues, if he has any, turn to vices by reason of the fact that they are his; work coming from his hands necessarily bears his stigma. If he builds a bridge, that bridge, being Jewish, is bad from the first to the last span. The same action carried out by a Jew and by a Christian does not have the same meaning in the two cases, for the Jew contaminates all that he touches with an I-know-not-what execrable quality. The first thing the Germans did was to forbid Jews access to swimming pools; it seemed to them that if the body of an Israelite were to plunge into that confined body of water, the water would be completely befouled. Strictly speaking, the Jew contaminates even the air he breathes.

If we attempt to formulate in abstract terms the principle to which the anti-Semite appeals, it would come to this: A whole is more and other than the sum of its parts; a whole determines the meaning and underlying character of the parts that make it up. There is not *one* virtue of courage which enters indifferently into a Jewish character or a Christian character in the way that oxygen indifferently combines with nitrogen and argon to form air and with hydrogen to form water. Each person is an indivisible totality that has its own courage, its own generosity, its own way of thinking, laughing, drinking, and eating. What is there to say except that the anti-Semite has chosen to fall back on the spirit of synthesis in order to understand the world. It is the spirit of synthesis which permits him to conceive of himself as forming an indissoluble unity with all France. It is in the name of this spirit that he denounces the purely analytical and critical intelligence of the Jews. But we must be more precise. For some time, on the Right and on the Left, among the traditionalists and among the socialists, it has been the fashion to make appeal to synthetic principles as against the spirit of analysis which presided over the foundation of bourgeois democracy. Yet both sides cannot be said to act on the same principles, or, if they do, they certainly make a different use of them. What use does the anti-Semite make of these principles?

We find scarcely any anti-Semitism among workers. It is absurd to answer that that is because there are no Jews in their ranks. Suppose the fact alleged were true; that is precisely what they would have to complain of. The Nazis knew it very well, for when they wished to extend their propaganda to the proletariat, they launched the slogan of "Jewish capitalism." The working class does, however, think about the social situation synthetically, only it does not use the methods of the anti-Semites. It sees ensembles in terms of economic functions. The bourgeoisie, the peasant class, the proletariat—those are the synthetic realities with which it is concerned, and in those complexes it distinguishes secondary synthetic structures—labor unions, employers' associations, trusts, cartels, parties. Thus the explanations it gives for historical phenomena are found to agree perfectly with the differentiated structure of a society based on division of labor. History, as the working class sees it, is the result of the play of economic organisms and the interaction of synthetic groups.

The majority of the anti-Semites, on the contrary, belongs to the middle class, that is, among men who have a level of life equal or superior to that of the Jews, or, if you prefer, among the "nonproducers" (employers, merchants, distributors, members of the liberal professions, parasites). The bourgeois in fact *does not produce:* he directs, administers, distributes, buys, sells. His function is to enter into direct relations with the consumer; in other words, his activity is based on a constant commerce with men, whereas the worker, in the exercise of his trade, is in permanent contact with things. Each man judges history in accordance with the profession that he follows. Shaped by the daily influence of the materials he works with, the workman sees society as the product of real forces acting in accordance with rigorous laws. His dialectical "materialism" signifies that he envisages the social world in the same way as the material world. On the other hand, the bourgeois—and the anti-Semite in particular—

have chosen to explain history by the action of individual wills. Do not the bourgeois depend on these same wills in the conduct of their affairs? * They behave toward social facts like primitives who endow the wind and the sun with little souls. Intrigues, cabals, the perfidy of one man, the courage and virtue of another —that is what determines the course of their business, that is what determines the course of the world. Anti-Semitism, a bourgeois phenomenon, appears therefore as a choice made to explain collective events by the initiative of individuals.

No doubt the proletarian caricatures "the bourgeois" on posters and in newspapers in exactly the same manner as the anti-Semite caricatures "the Jew." But this external resemblance should not deceive us. To the worker, what constitutes the bourgeois is his bourgeois status, that is, an ensemble of external factors; and the bourgeois himself is reducible to the synthetic unity of these externally apparent manifestations. It is an ensemble of various modes of *behavior*. For the anti-Semite, what makes the Jew is the presence in him of "Jewishness," a Jewish principle analogous to phlogiston or the soporific virtue of opium. We must not be

---

* I make an exception here of the engineer, the contractor, and the scientist, whose occupations bring them closer to the proletariat, and who in fact are infrequently anti-Semitic.

deceived: explanations on the basis of heredity and race came later; they are the slender scientific coating of this primitive conviction. Long before Mendel and Gobineau there was a horror of the Jew, and those who felt it could not explain it except by saying, like Montaigne of his friendship for La Boétie: "Because he is he, because I am I." Without the presence of this metaphysical essence, the activities ascribed to the Jew would be entirely incomprehensible. Indeed, how could we conceive of the obstinate folly of a rich Jewish merchant who, we are told, makes every effort to ruin his country, whereas if he were reasonable, he would desire the prosperity of the country in which he does business? How could we otherwise understand the evil internationalism of men whom their families, their affections, their habits, their interests, the nature and source of their fortunes should attach to the destiny of a particular country?

Facile talkers speak of a Jewish will to dominate the world. Here again, if we did not have the key, the manifestations of this will would certainly be unintelligible to us. We are told in almost the same breath that behind the Jew lurks international capitalism and the imperialism of the trusts and the munitions makers, and that he is the front man for piratical Bolshevism with a knife between its teeth. There is no embarrassment or hesitation about imputing responsibility for communism to Jewish bankers, whom it would horrify, or responsibility for capitalist imperialism to the wretched Jews who crowd the rue des Rosiers. But everything is made clear if we renounce any expectation from the Jew of a course of conduct that is reasonable and in conformity with his interests, if, instead, we discern in him a metaphysical principle that drives him *to do evil* under all circumstances, even though he thereby destroy himself. This principle, one may suspect, is magical. On the one hand, it is an essence, a substantial form, and the Jew, whatever he does, cannot modify it, any more than fire can keep itself from burning. On the other hand, it is necessary in order to be able to hate the Jew—for one does not hate natural phenomena like earthquakes and plagues of locusts—that it also have the virtue of freedom. Only the freedom in question is carefully limited: The Jew is free *to do evil*, not good; he has only as much free will as is necessary for him to take full responsibility for the crimes of which he is the author; he does not have enough to be able to achieve a reformation. Strange liberty, which instead of preceding and constituting the essence, remains subordinate to it, is only an irrational quality of it, and yet remains liberty.

There is only one creature, to my knowledge, who is

thus totally free and yet chained to evil; that is the Spirit of Evil himself, Satan. Thus the Jew is assimilable to the spirit of evil. His will, unlike the Kantian will, is one which wills itself purely, gratuitously, and universally to be evil. It is *the* will to evil. Through him Evil arrives on the earth. All that is bad in society (crises, wars, famines, upheavals, and revolts) is directly or indirectly imputable to him. The anti-Semite is afraid of discovering that the world is ill-contrived, for then it would be necessary for him to invent and modify, with the result that man would be found to be the master of his own destinies, burdened with an agonizing and infinite responsibility. Thus he localizes all the evil of the universe in the Jew. If nations war with each other, the conflict does not arise from the fact that the idea of nationality, in its present form, implies imperialism and the clash of interests. No, it is because the Jew is there, behind the governments, breathing discord. If there is a class struggle, it is not because the economic organization leaves something to be desired. It is because Jewish demagogues, hook-nosed agitators, have seduced the workers.

Anti-Semitism is thus seen to be at bottom a form of Manichaeism. It explains the course of the world by the struggle of the principle of Good with the principle of Evil. Between these two principles no reconciliation is conceivable; one of them must triumph and the other be annihilated. Look at Céline: his vision of the universe is catastrophic. The Jew is everywhere, the earth is lost, it is up to the Aryan not to compromise, never to make peace. Yet he must be on his guard: if he breathes, he has already lost his purity, for the very air that penetrates his bronchial tubes is contaminated. Does that not read like a diatribe by a Manichaean? If Céline supported the socialist theses of the Nazis, it was because he was paid to do so. At the bottom of his heart he did not believe in them. For him there is no solution except collective suicide, nonreproduction, death. Others—Maurras or the P. P. F.*—are less discouraging. They envisage a long and often doubtful struggle, with the final triumph of Good. It is Ormazd against Ahriman. The reader understands that the anti-Semite does not have recourse to Manichaeism as a secondary principle of explanation. It is the original choice he makes of Manichaeism which explains and conditions anti-Semitism. We must therefore ask ourselves what this original choice can mean for a man of today.

Let us compare for a moment the revolutionary idea of the class struggle with the Manichaeism of the anti-Semite. In the eyes of the Marxist, the class struggle is

* Parti Populaire Français.

41

in no sense a struggle between Good and Evil; it is a conflict of interests between human groups. The reason why the revolutionary adopts the point of view of the proletariat is, first of all, because it is *his own* class, then because it is oppressed, because it is by far the most numerous and consequently involves the fate of mankind in its own destiny, finally because the results of its victory will necessarily include the abolition of the class structure. The goal of the revolutionary is to change the organization of society. To do that it will no doubt be necessary to destroy the old regime. But that will not be sufficient; above all it will be necessary to build a new order. If by some impossible chance the privileged class were willing to co-operate in the social-ist reconstruction and gave clear proofs of its good faith, there would be no valid reason for repulsing it. If it is highly improbable that it will offer its support to the socialists in good faith, it is because its very situa-tion as a privileged class prevents it from doing so, not because of some indefinable interior demon which im-pels it to do evil in its own despite. In any case, if por-tions of this class break away from it, they can be con-stantly assimilated to the oppressed class, and they will be judged by their acts, not by their essence. "I don't give a damn for your eternal essence," Politzer told me one day.

42

On the other hand, the Manichaean anti-Semite puts his emphasis on destruction. What he sees is not a conflict of interests but the damage which an evil power causes society. Therefore Good consists above all in the destruction of Evil. Underneath the bitterness of the anti-Semite is concealed the optimistic belief that harmony will be re-established of itself, once Evil is eliminated. His task is therefore purely negative: there is no question of building a new society, but only of purifying the one which exists. In the attainment of this goal the co-operation of Jews of good will would be useless and even fatal, and anyhow no Jew could be a man of good will. Knight-errant of the Good, the anti-Semite is a holy man. The Jew also is holy in his manner— holy like the untouchables, like savages under the interdict of a taboo. Thus the conflict is raised to a religious plane, and the end of the combat can be nothing other than a holy destruction.

The advantages of this position are many. To begin with, it favors laziness of mind. We have seen that the anti-Semite understands nothing about modern society. He would be incapable of conceiving of a constructive plan; his action cannot reach the level of the methodical; it remains on the ground of passion. To a long-term enterprise he prefers an explosion of rage analogous to the running amuck of the Malays. His intellectual activity is confined to *interpretation;* he seeks in historical events the signs of the presence of an evil power. Out of this spring those childish and elaborate fabrications which give him his resemblance to the extreme paranoiacs. In addition, anti-Semitism channels revolutionary drives toward the destruction of certain men, not of institutions. An anti-Semitic mob will consider it has done enough when it has massacred some Jews and burned a few synagogues. It represents, therefore, a safety valve for the owning classes, who encourage it and thus substitute for a dangerous hate against their regime a beneficent hate against particular people. Above all this naive dualism is eminently reassuring to the anti-Semite himself. If all he has to do is to remove Evil, that means that the Good is already *given.* He has no need to seek it in anguish, to invent it, to scrutinize it patiently when he has found it, to prove it in action, to verify it by its consequences, or, finally, to shoulder the responsibilities of the moral choice he has made.

It is not by chance that the great outbursts of anti-Semitic rage conceal a basic optimism. The anti-Semite has cast his lot for Evil so as not to have to cast his lot for Good. The more one is absorbed in fighting Evil, the less one is tempted to place the Good in question. One does not need to talk about it, yet it is always understood in the discourse of the anti-Semite and it remains understood in his thought. When he has fulfilled his mission as holy destroyer, the Lost Paradise will reconstitute itself. For the moment so many tasks confront the anti-Semite that he does not have time to think about it. He is in the breach, fighting, and each of his outbursts of rage is a pretext to avoid the anguished search for the Good.

But that is not all, and now we touch on the domain of psychoanalysis. Manichaeism conceals a deep-seated attraction toward Evil. For the anti-Semite Evil is his lot, his Job's portion. Those who come after will concern themselves with the Good, if there is occasion. As for him, he is in the front rank of society, fighting with his back turned to the pure virtues that he defends. His business is with Evil; his duty is to unmask it, to denounce it, to measure its extent. That is why he is so obsessed with piling up anecdotes that reveal the lubricity of the Jew, his appetite for money, his ruses, and his treasons. He bathes his hands in ordure. Read again *La France Juive* of Drumont; that book of a "high French morality" is a collection of ignoble or obscene stories. Nothing reflects better the complex nature of the anti-Semite. Since through fear of standing out from the crowd he has not wished to *choose* his Good, allowing everybody else's to be imposed on him, his morality is never based on an intuition of values or on

45

what Plato calls Love. It shows itself only by the strict-est taboos, by the most rigorous and most gratuitous imperatives.

What he contemplates without intermission, that for which he has an intuition and almost a taste, is Evil. He can thus glut himself to the point of obsession with the recital of obscene or criminal actions which excite and satisfy his perverse leanings; but since at the same time he attributes them to those infamous Jews on whom he heaps his scorn, he satisfies himself without being com-promised. In Berlin I knew a Protestant in whom sexual desire took the form of indignation. The sight of women in bathing suits aroused him to fury; he willingly en-couraged that fury and passed his time at swimming pools. The anti-Semite is like that, and one of the ele-ments of his hatred is a profound sexual attraction to-ward Jews.

His behavior reflects a curiosity fascinated by Evil, but above all, I think, it represents a basic sadism. Anti-Semitism is incomprehensible unless one recalls that the Jew, object of so much execration, is perfectly inno-cent, I should even say inoffensive. Thus the anti-Semite takes pains to speak to us of secret Jewish organiza-tions, of formidable and clandestine freemasonries. Yet if he meets a Jew face to face, it is as often as not a weak creature who is ill-prepared to cope with violence and cannot even defend himself. The anti-Semite is well aware of this individual weakness of the Jew, which hands him over to pogroms with feet and hands bound —indeed, he licks his chops over it in advance. Thus his hatred for the Jew cannot be compared to that which the Italians of 1830 felt toward the Austrians, or that which the French of 1942 felt toward the Germans. In these instances it was a case of oppressors, of hard, cruel, and strong men who had arms, money, and power and who could do more harm to the rebels than the latter could have dreamed of doing to them. In hatreds like these sadistic leanings have no place. But since Evil, to the anti-Semite, is incarnated in unarmed and harmless men, the latter never finds himself under the painful necessity of being heroic. It is *fun* to be an anti-Semite. One can beat and torture Jews without fear. At most they can appeal to the laws of the Republic, but those laws are not too rigorous.

The sadistic attraction that the anti-Semite feels toward the Jew is so strong that it is not unusual to see one of these sworn enemies of Israel surround himself with Jewish friends. To be sure, he says they are "exceptional Jews," insists that "these aren't like the rest." (In the studio of the painter whom I mentioned earlier, a man who in no way spoke out against the butchery at Lublin, there was in full view the portrait of a Jew who was dear to him and whom the Gestapo had shot.) Such protestations of friendship are not sincere, for anti-Semites do not envisage, even in their statements, sparing the "good Jews," and, while they recognize some virtues in those whom they know, they will not admit that their interlocutors may have been able to meet others equally virtuous. Actually they take pleasure in protecting these few persons through a sort of inversion of their sadism; they take pleasure in keeping under their eyes the living image of this people whom they execrate. Anti-Semitic women often have a mixture of sexual repulsion and attraction toward Jews. One woman I knew had intimate relations with a Polish Jew. She would often go to bed with him and allow him to caress her breasts and shoulders, but nothing more. She enjoyed feeling him respectful and submissive, divining his violently frustrated and humiliated desire. She afterward had normal sexual intercourse with other men.

There is in the words "a beautiful Jewess" a very special sexual signification, one quite different from that contained in the words "beautiful Rumanian," "beautiful Greek," or "beautiful American," for example. This phrase carries an aura of rape and massacre. The "beautiful Jewess" is she whom the Cossacks under the czars dragged by her hair through the streets of her burning village. And the special works which are given over to accounts of flagellation reserve a place of honor for the Jewess. But it is not necessary to look into esoteric literature. From the Rebecca of *Ivanhoe* up to the Jewess of "Gilles," not forgetting the works of Ponson du Terrail, the Jewess has a well-defined function in even the most serious novels. Frequently violated or beaten, she sometimes succeeds in escaping dishonor by means of death, but that is a form of justice; and those who keep their virtue are docile servants or humiliated women in love with indifferent Christians who marry Aryan women. I think nothing more is needed to indicate the place the Jewess holds as a sexual symbol in folklore.

A destroyer in function, a sadist with a pure heart, the anti-Semite is, in the very depths of his heart, a criminal. What he wishes, what he prepares, is the *death* of the Jew.

To be sure, not all the enemies of the Jew demand his death openly, but the measures they propose—all of which aim at his abasement, at his humiliation, at his banishment—are substitutes for that assassination which they meditate within themselves. They are symbolic murders. Only, the anti-Semite has his conscience on his side: he is a criminal in a good cause. It is not his fault, surely, if his mission is to extirpate Evil by doing

49

Evil. The *real* France has delegated to him the powers of her High Court of Justice. No doubt he does not have occasion every day to make use of them, but we should not be misled on that account. These sudden fits of anger which seize him, these thundering diatribes which he hurls at the "Yids" are so many capital executions. The anti-Semite has chosen to be a criminal, and a criminal *pure of heart*. Here again he flees responsibilities. Though he censures his murderous instincts, he has found a means of sating them without admitting it to himself. He knows that he is wicked, but since he does Evil *for the sake of Good*, since a whole people waits for deliverance at his hands, he looks upon himself as a sanctified evildoer. By a sort of inversion of all values, of which we find examples in certain religions —for example, in India, where there exists a sacred prostitution—the anti-Semite accords esteem, respect, and enthusiasm to anger, hate, pillage, murder, to all the forms of violence. Drunk with evil, he feels in himself the lightness of heart and peace of mind which a good conscience and the satisfaction of a duty well done bring.

The portrait is complete. If some of those who readily assert that they detest the Jews do not recognize themselves in it, it is because in actual fact they do not detest the Jews. They don't love them either. While they would not do them the least harm, they would not raise their little fingers to protect them from violence. They are not anti-Semites. They are not anything; they are not *persons*. Since it is necessary to appear to be something, they make themselves into an echo, a murmur, and, without thinking of evil—without thinking of anything —they go about repeating learned formulas which give them the right of entry to certain drawing rooms. Thus they know the delights of being nothing but an empty noise, of having their heads filled with an enormous affirmation which they find all the more respectable because they have borrowed it. Anti-Semitism is only a justification for their existence. Their futility is such that they will eagerly abandon this justification for any other, provided that the latter be more "distinguished." For anti-Semitism is *distinguished*, as are all the manifestations of a collective and irrational soul which seek to create an occult and conservative France. It seems to all these featherbrains that by repeating with eager emulation the statement that the Jew is harmful to the country they are performing a rite of initiation which admits them to the fireside of social warmth and energy. In this sense anti-Semitism has kept something of the nature of human sacrifice.

It has, moreover, a considerable advantage for those people who are aware of their profound instability and are weary of it. It permits them to put on the externals of passion and, as has been fashionable since the Romantic movement, to confuse this with personality. These secondhand anti-Semites can provide themselves at little cost with an aggressive personality. One of my friends often used to tell me about an elderly cousin of his who came to dine with his family and about whom they said, with a certain air: "Jules can't abide the English." My friend doesn't recall that they ever said anything else about Cousin Jules. But that was enough. There was a tacit understanding between Jules and his family: They ostentatiously avoided talking about the English in front of him, and that precaution gave him a semblance of existence in the eyes of those about him at the same time that it provided them with the agreeable sensation of participating in a sacred ceremony. Then on occasion after careful deliberation, someone, as if by inadvertence, would throw out an allusion to Great Britain or her dominions. Cousin Jules, pretending to become very angry, would feel himself come to life for a moment, and everybody would be happy. Many people are anti-Semites in the way Cousin Jules was an Anglophobe, without, to be sure, realizing the true implications of their attitude. Pale reflections, reeds shaken by the wind, they certainly would not have invented anti-Semitism, if the conscious anti-Semite did not already exist. But it is they who with complete indifference assure the survival of anti-Semitism and carry it forward through the generations.

We are now in a position to understand the anti-Semite. He is a man who is afraid. Not of the Jews, to be sure, but of himself, of his own consciousness, of his liberty, of his instincts, of his responsibilities, of solitariness, of change, of society, and of the world—of everything except the Jews. He is a coward who does not want to admit his cowardice to himself; a murderer who represses and censures his tendency to murder without being able to hold it back, yet who dares to kill only in effigy or protected by the anonymity of the mob; a malcontent who dares not revolt from fear of the consequences of his rebellion. In espousing anti-Semitism, he does not simply adopt an opinion, he chooses himself as a person. He chooses the permanence and impenetrability of stone, the total irresponsibility of the warrior who obeys his leaders—and he has no leader. He chooses to acquire nothing, to deserve nothing; he assumes that everything is given him as his birthright—and he is not noble. He chooses finally a Good that is fixed once and for all, beyond question, out of reach; he dares not examine it for fear of being led to challenge it and having to seek it in another form. The Jew only serves him as a pretext; elsewhere his counterpart will make use of the Negro or the man of yellow skin. The existence of the Jew merely permits the anti-Semite to stifle his anxieties at their inception by persuading himself that his place in the world has been marked out in advance, that it awaits him, and that tradition gives him the right to occupy it. Anti-Semitism, in short, is fear of the human condition. The anti-Semite is a man who wishes to be pitiless stone, a furious torrent, a devastating thunderbolt—anything except a man.

2

The Jews have one friend, however, the democrat. But he is a feeble protector. No doubt he proclaims that all men have equal rights; no doubt he has founded the League for the Rights of Man; but his own declarations show the weakness of his position. In the eighteenth century, once and for all, he made his choice: the analytic spirit. He has no eyes for the concrete syntheses with which history confronts him. He recognizes neither Jew, nor Arab, nor Negro, nor bourgeois, nor worker, but only man—man always the same in all times and all places. He resolves all collectivities into individual elements. To him a physical body is a collection of molecules; a social body, a collection of individuals. And by individual he means the incarnation in a single example of the universal traits which make up human nature.

Thus the anti-Semite and the democrat tirelessly carry on their dialogue without ever understanding one another or realizing that they are not talking about the same things. If the anti-Semite reproaches the Jew for his avarice, the democrat will reply that he knows Jews who are not avaricious and Christians who are. But the anti-Semite is not moved. What he meant was that there is a "Jewish" avarice, an avarice determined by that synthetic whole, the Jewish *person*. He can agree without embarrassment that it is possible for certain Christians to be avaricious, for to him Christian avarice and Jewish avarice are not the same. To the democrat, on the contrary, avarice has a certain universal and invariable nature that can be added to the ensemble of the traits which make up an individual and still remain the same under all circumstances. There are not two ways of being avaricious: one is or one is not.

The democrat, like the scientist, fails to see the particular case; to him the individual is only an ensemble of universal traits. It follows that his defense of the Jew saves the latter as man and annihilates him as Jew. In contrast to the anti-Semite, the democrat is not afraid of himself; what he fears is the great collective forms in which he is in danger of being disintegrated. Thus he has chosen to throw in his lot with the analytic spirit because it does not see these synthetic realities. Taking this point of view, he fears the awakening of a "Jewish consciousness" in the Jew; that is, he fears that the Jew will acquire a consciousness of the Jewish collectivity

56

—just as he fears that a "class conciousness" may awaken in the worker. His defense is to persuade individuals that they exist in an isolated state. "There are no Jews," he says, "there is no Jewish question." This means that he wants to separate the Jew from his religion, from his family, from his ethnic community, in order to plunge him into the democratic crucible whence he will emerge naked and alone, an individual and solitary particle like all the other particles.

This is what, in the United States, is called the policy of assimilation; immigration laws have registered the failure of this policy and, on the whole, the failure of the democratic point of view. How could it be otherwise? For a Jew, conscious and proud of being Jewish, asserting his claim to be a member of the Jewish community without ignoring on that account the bonds which unite him to the national community, there may not be so much difference between the anti-Semite and the democrat. The former wishes to destroy him as a man and leave nothing in him but the Jew, the pariah, the untouchable; the latter wishes to destroy him as a Jew and leave nothing in him but the man, the abstract and universal subject of the rights of man and the rights of the citizen.

Thus there may be detected in the most liberal democrat a tinge of anti-Semitism; he is hostile to the Jew to the extent that the latter thinks of himself as a Jew. He expresses this hostility by a sort of indulgent and amused irony, as when he says of a Jewish friend whose Semitic origin is easily recognizable: "Just the same, he is *too* Jewish." Or when he declares: "The only thing I have against the Jews is their clannishness; if you let one in, he will bring ten more with him." During the Occupation the democrat was profoundly and sincerely indignant at the anti-Semitic persecutions, but he sighed from time to time: "The Jews will come back from exile with such insolence and hunger for vengeance that I am afraid of a new outburst of anti-Semitism." What he really feared was that the persecutions might have helped to give the Jew a more definite consciousness of himself.

The anti-Semite reproaches the Jew with *being* Jewish; the democrat reproaches him with wilfully *considering himself* a Jew. Between his enemy and his defender, the Jew is in a difficult situation: apparently he can do no more than choose the sauce with which he will be devoured. We must now ask ourselves the question: does the Jew exist? And if he exists, what is he? Is he first a Jew or first a man? Is the solution of the problem to be found in the extermination of all the Israelites or in their total assimilation? Or is it possible to find some other way of stating the problem and of resolving it?

3

We are in agreement with the anti-Semite on one point: we do not believe in "human nature"; we cannot conceive of society as a sum of isolated molecules; we believe that it is necessary to consider biological, psychical, and social phenomena in a spirit of synthesis. But we take leave of the anti-Semite when it comes to applying this spirit of synthesis. We certainly do not know of any Jewish "principle," and we are not Manichaeans. Neither do we admit that the "true" Frenchman benefits so readily from the experience or the traditions left him by his ancestors; we remain highly sceptical on the subject of psychological heredity, and we are willing to utilize ethnic concepts only in the areas where they have received experimental confirmation—in biology and pathology, for example.

For us, man is defined first of all as a being "in a situation." That means that he forms a synthetic whole with his situation—biological, economic, political, cultural, etc. He cannot be distinguished from his situation, for it forms him and decides his possibilities; but, inversely, it is he who gives it meaning by making his choices within it and by it. To be in a situation, as we see it, is *to choose oneself* in a situation, and men differ from one another in their situations and also in the choices they themselves make of themselves. What men have in common is not a "nature" but a condition, that is, an ensemble of limits and restrictions: the inevitability of death, the necessity of working for a living, of living in a world already inhabited by other men. Fundamentally this condition is nothing more than the basic human situation, or, if you prefer, the ensemble of abstract characteristics common to all situations. I agree therefore with the democrat that the Jew is a man like other men, but this tells me nothing in particular —except that he is free, that he is at the same time in bondage, that he is born, enjoys life, suffers, and dies, that he loves and hates, just as do all men. I can derive nothing more from these excessively general data. If I wish to know *who* the Jew is, I must first inquire into the situation surrounding him, since he is a being in a situation. I give warning that I shall limit my description to the Jews in France, for it is the problem of the French Jew that is *our* problem.

I shall not deny that there is a Jewish race. But we

60

must understand each other at once. If by "race" is understood that indefinable complex into which are tossed pell-mell both somatic characteristics and intellectual and moral traits, I believe in it no more than I do in ouija boards. What, for lack of a better term, I shall call ethnic characteristics, are certain inherited physical conformations that one encounters more frequently among Jews than among non-Jews. Here it is still advisable to be prudent: perhaps we had better say Jewish *races*. We know that not all Semites are Jews, which complicates the problem. We also know that certain blond Jews of Russia are still further removed from the woolly-headed Jews of Algeria than from the "Aryans" of East Prussia. As a matter of fact, each country has its Jews and our picture of an Israelite hardly corresponds at all to our neighbors' picture.

When I lived in Berlin at the beginning of the Nazi regime, I had two French friends one of whom was a Jew and one of whom was not. The Jew was of a "marked Semitic type": he had a hooked nose, protruding ears, and thick lips. A Frenchman would have recognized him as a Jew without hesitation. But since he was blond, lean, and phlegmatic, the Germans were completely taken in. He occasionally amused himself by going out with SS men, who did not suspect his race. One of them said to him one day: "I can tell a Jew a hundred yards off." My other friend was a Corsican and a Catholic, the son and grandson of Catholics, but he had hair that was black and a bit curly, a Bourbon nose, a sallow complexion, and he was short and fat. The children in the street threw stones at him and called him "Jude." That was because he closely resembled a certain type of Eastern Jew who is most popular in the German stereotype.

However that may be, even admitting that all Jews have certain physical traits in common, it would be rash to conclude from that, unless by the vaguest of analogies, that they must also show the same traits of character. Or better: the physical stigmata which one can observe in the Semite are spatial, therefore juxtaposed and separable. I can on a moment's notice find any one of them in an "Aryan." Am I to conclude, then, that this "Aryan" has such and such a psychic quality which is ordinarily attributed to Jews? Evidently not. But in that case the whole theory crumbles. It presupposes that the Jew is an indivisible totality, whereas we have just shown him to be a mosaic in which each element is a pebble that we can take out and place in another pattern. Thus we can neither deduce the moral from the physical nor postulate a psycho-physiological parallelism. If I am told that I must consider the ensemble of somatic characteristics, I will reply: Either this ensemble is the *sum* of ethnic traits and that sum can in no way represent the spatial equivalent of a psychic *synthesis*—any more than an association of cerebral cells can correspond to a thought—or when we speak of the physical aspect of a Jew, we understand a syncretic totality that yields to intuition. In this case, to be sure, there may be a *Gestalt* in the sense in which Koehler understands the word, and it is to this that the anti-Semites allude when they pretend to "smell a Jew," "have a feel for a Jew," etc., etc. Only, it is impossible to perceive somatic elements apart from the psychic signification which is mingled with them.

Here is a Jew seated on his doorstep in the rue des Rosiers. I recognize him immediately as a Jew: he has a black and curly beard, a slightly hooked nose, protruding ears, steel-rimmed glasses, a derby pulled down over his eyes, black clothes, quick and nervous gestures, and a smile of strange and dolorous goodness. How am I to disentangle the physical from the moral? His beard is black and curly; that is a somatic characteristic. But what strikes me above all is that he lets it grow; by that he expresses his attachment to the traditions of the Jewish community; he indicates that he has come from Poland, that he belongs to emigrants of the first generation. Is his son any less a Jew for being clean-shaven? Other traits, like the form of his nose and the position of his ears, are purely anatomical, while others, like the choice of clothing and glasses, expression and mimicry, are purely psychical and social. What is it then that reveals this man to me as an Israelite, if not this inseparable ensemble in which the psychical and the physical, the social, the religious, and the individual are closely mingled, if not this living synthesis that evidently could not be transmitted by heredity and which, at bottom, is identical with his complete personality? We must therefore envisage the hereditary and somatic characteristics of the Jew as one factor among others in his situation, not as a condition determining his nature.

Failing to determine the Jew by his race, shall we define him by his religion or by the existence of a strictly Israelite national community? Here the question becomes complicated. Certainly at a remote time in the past there was a religious and national community that was called Israel. But the history of that community is one of dissolution over a period of twenty-five centuries. First it lost its sovereignty; there was the Babylonian captivity, then the Persian domination, finally the Roman conquest. We must not see in this the effect of a curse—unless there are geographical curses. The situation of Palestine, crossroads for all the commercial routes of the ancient world, and crushed between mighty empires, is sufficient to explain this slow loss of power. The religious bond was strengthened between the Jews of the dispersion and those who remained on their own soil; it took on the sense and value of a national bond. But this "transfer," it is to be suspected, indicated a spiritualization of collective ties, and spiritualization, after all, means enfeeblement. Shortly after this, moreover, the introduction of Christianity brought division; the appearance of this new religion caused a great crisis in the Israelite world, setting the Jewish emigrants against those remaining in Judea. In contrast to the "strong form" that Christianity was from the first, the Hebraic religion appeared immediately as a weak form, on the road to disintegration. It managed to maintain itself only by a complicated policy of concessions and obstinacy. It resisted the persecutions and the dispersion of the Jews in the medieval world; it much less effectively resisted the progress of enlightenment and the critical spirit.

The Jews who surround us today have only a ceremonial and polite contact with their religion. I once asked one of them why he had his son circumcised. He replied: "Because it pleased my mother, and because it's the right thing to do." "And why does your mother hold to it?" "Because of her friends and neighbors." I realize that these overly rational explanations conceal a secret and deep-seated need to attach oneself to tradition and, in default of a national past, to give oneself roots in a past of rites and customs. But that is just the point: religion is here only a symbolic means. At least in Western Europe the Jewish religion has been unable to resist the attacks launched by rationalism and by the Christian spirit; atheistic Jews whom I have questioned admit that their dialogue on the existence of God is carried on against the Christian religion. The religion which they attack and of which they wish to rid themselves is Christianity; their atheism differs in no way from that of a Roger Martin du Gard, who says he has disengaged himself from the Catholic faith. Not for a moment are Jews atheistic against the Talmud; and priest, to all of them, means the vicar, not the rabbi.

Thus the facts of the problem appear as follows: a concrete historical community is basically *national* and *religious;* but the Jewish community, which once was both, has been deprived bit by bit of both these concrete characteristics. We may call it an abstract historical community. Its dispersion implies the breaking up of common traditions, and it was remarked above that its twenty centuries of dispersion and political impotence forbid its having a *historic past.* If it is true, as Hegel says, that a community is historical to the degree that it remembers its history, then the Jewish community is the least historical of all, for it keeps a memory of nothing but a long martyrdom, that is, of a long passivity.

What is it, then, that serves to keep a semblance of unity in the Jewish community? To reply to this question, we must come back to the idea of *situation*. It is neither their past, their religion, nor their soil that unites the sons of Israel. If they have a common bond, if all of them deserve the name of Jew, it is because they have in common the situation of a Jew, that is, they live in a community which takes them for Jews.

In a word, the Jew is perfectly assimilable by modern nations, but he is to be defined as one whom these nations do not wish to assimilate. What weighed upon him originally was that he was the assassin of Christ.* Have we ever stopped to consider the intolerable situation of men condemned to live in a society that adores the God they have killed? Originally, the Jew was therefore a murderer or the son of a murderer—which in the eyes of a community with a pre-logical concept of responsibility amounts inevitably to the same thing —it was as such that he was taboo. It is evident that we

----

* We must take note at once that it is a question here of a legend created by Christian propaganda during the dispersion. It is evident that the cross is a *Roman* instrument of torture and that Christ was executed *by the Romans* as a political agitator.

cannot find the explanation for modern anti-Semitism here; but if the anti-Semite has chosen the Jew as the object of his hate, it is because of the religious horror that the latter has always inspired.

This horror has had a curious economic effect. If the medieval church tolerated the Jews when she could have assimilated them by force or massacred them, it was because they filled a vital economic function. Accursed, they followed a cursed but indispensable vocation; being unable to own land or serve in the army, they trafficked in money, which a Christian could not undertake without defiling himself. Thus the original curse was soon reinforced by an economic curse, and it is above all the latter that has persisted. Today we reproach the Jews for following unproductive activities, without taking into account the fact that their apparent autonomy within the nation comes from the fact that they were originally forced into these trades by being forbidden all others. Thus it is no exaggeration to say that it is the Christians who have *created* the Jew in putting an abrupt stop to his assimilation and in providing him, in spite of himself, with a function in which he has since prospered.

Here, too, there is really only a memory; differentiation of economic functions is such today that one cannot assign the Jew a very definite sphere of activity; at most it might be noticed that his long exclusion from certain trades has diverted him from them even when he has had the chance to engage in them. But modern society has seized on this memory and has made it the pretext and the base for its anti-Semitism. Thus, to know what the contemporary Jew is, we must ask the Christian conscience. And we must ask, not "What is a Jew?" but *"What have you made of the Jews?"*

The Jew is one whom other men consider a Jew: that is the simple truth from which we must start. In this sense the democrat is right as against the anti-Semite, for it is the anti-Semite who *makes* the Jew. But it would be wrong to say that the distrust, the curiosity, the disguised hostility the Israelites find around them are no more than the intermittent demonstrations of a few hotheads. Primarily, as we have seen, anti-Semitism is the expression of a primitive society that, though secret and diffused, remains latent in the legal collectivity. We must not suppose, therefore, that a generous outburst of emotion, a few pretty words, a stroke of the pen will suffice to suppress it. That would be like imagining you could abolish war by denouncing its effects in a book.

The Jew no doubt sets a proper value on the sympathy shown him, but it cannot prevent his seeing anti-Semitism as a permanent structure of the community

69

in which he lives. He knows, moreover, that the democrats and all those who defend him have a tendency to treat anti-Semitism rather leniently. First of all, we live in a republic, where all opinions are free. In addition, the myth of national unity still exerts such an influence over the French that they are ready for the greatest compromises in order to avoid internal conflict, especially in periods of international tension—which are, of course, precisely those when anti-Semitism is the most violent. Naive and full of good will, it is inevitably the democrat who makes all the concessions; the anti-Semite doesn't make any. He has the advantage of his anger. People say, "Don't irritate him." They speak softly in his presence.

In 1940, for example, many Frenchmen went over to the side of the Pétain government, which did not fail to preach unity—we know with what reservations. This government initiated anti-Semitic measures. The "Pétainists" did not protest. They felt extremely ill at ease, but what was to be done? If France could be saved at the cost of a few sacrifices, was it not better to close one's eyes? Certainly these people were not anti-Semites; they even spoke to the Jews whom they met with commiseration and politeness. But how could these Jews not realize that they were being sacrificed to the mirage of a united and patriarchal France?

Today * those Jews whom the Germans did not deport or murder are coming back to their homes. Many were among the first members of the Resistance; others had sons or cousins in Leclerc's army. Now all France rejoices and fraternizes in the streets; social conflict seems temporarily forgotten; the newspapers devote whole columns to stories of prisoners of war and deportees. Do we say anything about the Jews? Do we give a thought to those who died in the gas chambers at Lublin? Not a word. Not a line in the newspapers. That is because we must not irritate the anti-Semites; more than ever, we need unity. Well-meaning journalists will tell you: "In the interest of the Jews themselves, it would not do to talk too much about them just now." For four years French society has lived without them; it is just as well not to emphasize too vigorously the fact that they have reappeared.

Does anyone think that the Jews don't know what is happening, that they don't understand the reasons for this silence? Some of them approve, and say: "The less we are noticed, the better." Can a Frenchman, sure of himself, of his religion, of his race, possibly understand the state of mind that dictates such a statement? Is it not plain that to have arrived at this resigned wisdom, at this policy of self-effacement, the Jews must for years

* Written in October 1944.

have been fully aware of hostility, ugly looks always watching, indifference always ready to turn into bitterness—this in their own country? Thus they have made a clandestine return, and their joy at being liberated is not part of the nation's joy. The following little anecdote will serve to show what they have suffered on this account. In my *Lettres Françaises* without thinking about it particularly, and simply for the sake of completeness, I wrote something or other about the sufferings of the prisoners of war, the deportees, the political prisoners, and the Jews. Several Jews thanked me in a most touching manner. How completely must they have felt themselves abandoned, to think of thanking an author for merely having written the word "Jew" in an article!

Thus the Jew is in the situation of a Jew because he lives in the midst of a society that takes him for a Jew. He has passionate enemies, and defenders lacking in passion. The democrat professes moderation; he blames or admonishes while synagogues are being set on fire. He is tolerant by profession; he is, indeed, snobbish about tolerance and even extends it to the enemies of democracy. Wasn't it the style among radicals of the Left to consider Maurras a genius? How can the democrat fail to understand the anti-Semite! It is as if he were fascinated by all who plot his downfall. Perhaps at the bottom of his heart he yearns after the violence which he has denied himself.

In any case, the struggle is not equal. If the democrat were to put some warmth into pleading the cause of the Jew, he would have to be a Manichaean too, and equate the Jew with the principle of the Good. But how could he do this? The democrat is not a fool. He makes himself the advocate of the Jew because he sees him as a member of humanity; since humanity has other members whom he must also defend, the democrat has much to do; he concerns himself with the Jew when he has time. But the anti-Semite has only one enemy, and he can think of him all the time. Thus it is he who calls the turn. Vigorously attacked, feebly defended, the Jew feels himself in danger in a society in which anti-Semitism is the continual temptation. This is what we must look at more closely.

The French Jews are for the most part members of the lower or upper middle class. In general, they follow vocations I shall call vocations of opinion, in the sense that success depends not on their skill in working with materials but in the opinion that other men have of them. Whether a man is a lawyer or a haberdasher, his clientele comes if he is pleasing. It follows that the vocations of which we are speaking are full of ceremonies; it is necessary to seduce, to captivate, and to retain confidence. Correctness of costume, apparent severity of conduct, honor, all are based on these ceremonies, on the thousand little dance steps it is necessary to take in order to attract a customer. Thus what counts above all else is reputation. A man *makes* himself a reputation, he lives on it; that means that basically he is completely dependent on other men, whereas the peasant has primarily to do with his land, the worker with his materials and tools.

The Jew thus finds himself in a paradoxical situation: it is perfectly all right for him to gain a reputation for honesty, just as others do and in the same ways, but this reputation is added to a primary reputation—that of being a Jew—which has been imposed on him at one stroke and from which he cannot free himself no matter what he may do. The Jewish workman in the mine, in the foundry, at the wheel of a truck, can forget that he is a Jew; the Jewish businessman cannot forget it. Let him multiply acts of disinterestedness and honesty, and perhaps he will be called a *good* Jew. But Jew he is and must remain.

At least when he is called honest or dishonest, he knows what it is about; he remembers the acts that justify these terms. When he is called Jew, it is quite otherwise; then it is a question not of a particular condition but of a certain tone expressed in all his actions.

He has heard repeatedly that a Jew thinks like a Jew, sleeps, drinks, eats like a Jew, is honest or dishonest in a Jewish manner. And the Jew looks for this Jewishness in vain. Is any of us conscious of his style of behavior? Can any of us look at himself from the outside?

Yet this little word "Jew" appears in his life one fine day and will never leave again. Some children by the time they are six have already had fights with schoolmates who call them "Yids." Others may remain in ignorance for a long time. A young Jewish girl in a family I am acquainted with did not even know the meaning of the word Jew until she was fifteen. During the Occupation there was a Jewish doctor who lived shut up in his home at Fontainebleau and raised his children without saying a word to them of their origin. But however it comes about, some day they must learn the truth: sometimes from the smiles of those who surround them, sometimes from rumor or insult. The later the discovery, the more violent the shock. Suddenly they perceive that others know something about them that they don't know, that people apply to them an ugly and upsetting term that is not used in their own family. They feel themselves separated, cut off from the society of the normal children who run and play tranquilly and securely around them—those lucky children who have no *special name*. And they return home, they look at their father, they think: "Is he a Jew too?" How can they fail to keep the marks of this first revelation all their lives? There have been hundreds of descriptions of the disturbances which occur in a child when he suddenly discovers that his parents have sexual relations. But what must happen to the little Jew when he steals a glance at his parents and thinks: "They are Jews"?

At home, he is told that he should be proud of being a Jew. And he no longer knows what to believe; he is torn between humiliation, anguish, and pride. He feels that he is set apart, but he still does not understand what sets him apart; he is sure of only one thing: no matter what he does, he is and will remain a Jew.

We have been indignant, and rightly, over the obscene "yellow star" that the German government forced upon the Jews. What seemed intolerable about this was that it called attention to the Jew, that it obliged him to feel himself perpetually Jewish in the eyes of others. There were some who tried by all possible means to indicate their sympathy for the unfortunates so marked. But when very well-intentioned people undertook to raise their hats to Jews whom they encountered, the Jews themselves felt that these salutes were extremely painful. Under the looks of support and compassion, they felt themselves becoming *objects:* objects of commiseration, of pity, of what you will—but objects. They provided these virtuous liberals with an occasion for making a general gesture, for uttering a manifesto. They were only an occasion.

The liberal, when he met a Jew, was free, completely free to shake his hand or spit in his face; he could decide in accordance with his morality, with the way he had chosen to be; but the Jew was not free to be a Jew. Thus the strongest souls among the Jews preferred the gesture of hate to the gesture of charity, because hate is a passion and seems less free, whereas charity manifests itself from above to those below. In the end we came to understand all this so well that we turned our eyes away when we met a Jew wearing a star. We were ill at ease, embarrassed by our own glance, which, if it fell upon him, made him a Jew in spite of himself and in spite of ourselves. The supreme expression of sympathy and of friendship lay here in appearing to ignore, for whatever effort we made to reach to the *person*, it was always the *Jew* whom we encountered.

Yet the Nazi ordinances only carried to its extreme a situation to which we had formerly accommodated ourselves very well. Before the armistice, to be sure, the Jew did not wear a star. But his name, his face, his gestures, and a thousand other traits designated him as a Jew; walking in the streets, entering a café, a store, a

77

drawing room, he knew himself *marked* as a Jew. If someone approached him with a manner a little too open and too friendly, he knew at once that he had become the object of a demonstration of tolerance, that his interlocutor had chosen him as a pretext for declaring to the world, and to himself: "Look at me, I have liberal ideas, I am not an anti-Semite, I know only individuals, not races."

But within himself, the Jew considers himself the same as others. He speaks the same language; he has the same class interests, the same national interests; he reads the newspapers that the others read, he votes as they do, he understands and shares their opinions. Yet they give him to understand that he does not belong, that he has a "Jewish way" of speaking, of reading, of voting. And if he asks for an explanation, they sketch a portrait in which he does not recognize himself. There can be no doubt of its being his portrait, since millions of people maintain that it is. What can he do? We shall see later on that the root of Jewish disquietude is the necessity imposed upon the Jew of subjecting himself to endless self-examination and finally of assuming a phantom personality, at once strange and familiar, that haunts him and which is nothing but himself—himself as others see him. You may say that this is the lot of all, that each of us has a character familiar to those

78

close to us which we ourselves do not see. No doubt: this is the expression of our fundamental relation to the Other. But the Jew has a personality like the rest of us, and on top of that he is Jewish. It amounts in a sense to a doubling of the fundamental relationship with the Other. The Jew is over-determined.

What, in his eyes, makes his situation even more incomprehensible is that he has the full enjoyment of his rights as a citizen, at least so long as the society in which he lives is in equilibrium. In periods of crisis and of persecution, he is a hundred times more unhappy, but at least he can revolt, and, by a dialectic analogous to that which Hegel describes in his *Master and Slave*, he can regain his liberty by opposing oppression and denying his accursed "Jewish nature" in armed resistance against those who wish to impose it on him.

But when all is calm, against whom is he to revolt? He accepts the society around him, he joins the game and he conforms to all the ceremonies, dancing with the others the dance of respectability. Besides, he is nobody's slave; he is a free citizen under a regime that allows free competition; he is forbidden no social dignity, no office of the state. He may be decorated with the ribbon of the Legion of Honor, he may become a great lawyer or a cabinet minister. But at the very moment when he reaches the summits of legal society, another society—amorphous, diffused, and omnipresent —appears before him as if in brief flashes of lightning and refuses to take him in. How sharply must he feel the vanity of honors and of fortune, when the greatest success will never gain him entrance into that society which considers itself the "real" one. As a cabinet minister, he will be a Jewish cabinet minister, at once an "Excellency" and an untouchable. And yet he never encounters any particular resistance; people seem, rather, to be in flight before him; an impalpable chasm widens out, and, above all, an invisible chemistry devaluates all that he touches.

In a bourgeois society it is the constant movement of people, the collective currents, the styles, the customs, all these things, that in effect create *values*. The values of poems, of furniture, of houses, of landscapes derive in large part from the spontaneous condensations that fall on these objects like a light dew; they are strictly national and result from the normal functioning of a traditionalist and historical society. To be a Frenchman is not merely to have been born in France, to vote and pay taxes; it is above all to have the use and the sense of these values. And when a man shares in their creation, he is in some degree reassured about himself; he has a justification for existence through a sort of adhesion to the whole of society. To know how to appreciate a piece of Louis Seize furniture, the delicacy of a saying by Chamfort, a landscape of the Ile de France, a painting by Claude Lorrain, is to affirm and to feel that one belongs to French society; it is to renew a tacit social contract with all the members of that society. At one stroke the vague contingency of our existence vanishes and gives way to the necessity of an existence by right. Every Frenchman who is moved by reading Villon or by looking at the Palace of Versailles becomes a public functionary and the subject of imprescriptible rights.

Now a Jew is a man who is refused access to these values on principle. No doubt the worker is in the same predicament, but his situation is different. He can disdainfully reject the values and the culture of the middle class; he can dream of substituting his own. The Jew, in theory, belongs to the very class of people who reject him; he shares their tastes and their way of life. He *touches* these values but he does not see them; they should be his and they are refused him. He is told that he is blind. Naturally that is false. Are we to believe that Bloch, Crémieux, Suarès, Schwob, Benda understand the great French masterpieces less well than a Christian grocer or a Christian policeman? Are we to believe that Max Jacob was less competent to handle our language than an "Aryan" municipal clerk? And

Proust, a half-Jew, did he understand Racine only half-way? As between the "Aryan" Chuquet, celebrated for his bad style, and the Jew Léon Blum, which one has understood Stendhal the better?

But it is of no importance that this is an erroneous notion; the fact is that it is a group error. The Jew must decide for himself whether it is true or false; indeed he must prove it. And yet people will always reject the proof which he furnishes. He may go as far as he wants in understanding a work of art, a custom, a period, a style. What constitutes the *true* value of the object considered, a value accessible only to Frenchmen of the "real" France, is exactly that which is "beyond" and which cannot be expressed in words. In vain may he argue about his culture, his accomplishments; it is a Jewish culture; they are Jewish accomplishments. He is a Jew precisely in that he does not even suspect what ought to be understood. Thus an attempt is made to persuade him that the true sense of things must always escape him; there is formed around him an impalpable atmosphere, which is the *genuine* France, with its *genuine* values, its *genuine* tact, its *genuine* morality, and he has no part in it.

He can, indeed, acquire all the goods he wants, lands and castles if he has the wherewithal; but at the very moment when he becomes a legal proprietor, the property undergoes a subtle change in meaning and value. Only a Frenchman, the son of a Frenchman, son or grandson of a peasant, is capable of possessing it really. To own a hut in a village, it is not enough to have bought it with hard cash. One must know all the neighbors, their parents and grandparents, the surrounding farms, the beeches and oaks of the forest; one must know how to work, fish, hunt; one must have made notches in the trees in childhood and have found them enlarged in ripe old age. You may be sure that the Jew does not fulfil these conditions. For that matter, perhaps the Frenchman doesn't either, but he is granted a certain indulgence. There is a French way and a Jewish way of confusing oats and wheat.

Thus the Jew remains the stranger, the intruder, the unassimilated at the very heart of our society. Everything is accessible to him, and yet he possesses nothing; for, he is told, what one possesses is not to be bought. All that he touches, all that he acquires becomes devaluated in his hands; the goods of the earth, the true goods, are always those which he has not. He is well aware that he has contributed as much as another to forging the future of the society that rejects him. But if the future is to be his, at least he is refused the past. If he turns toward the past, he sees that his race has no part in it. Call the roll of the kings of France, their ministers, their great captains, the artists, the men of learning—none were Jews. And Jews did not bring about the French Revolution.

The reason for all this is simple. Until the nineteenth century the Jews, like women, were in a state of tutelage; thus their contribution to political and social life, like that of women, is of recent date. The names of Einstein, of Bergson, of Chagall, of Kafka are enough to show what they would have been able to bring to the world if they had been emancipated earlier. But that is of no importance; the fact is there. These are Frenchmen who have no part in the history of France. Their collective memory furnishes them only with obscure recollections of pogroms, of ghettos, of exoduses, of great monotonous sufferings, twenty centuries of repetition, not of evolution. The Jew is not yet *historical*, and yet he is the most ancient of peoples, or nearly so. That is what gives him the air of being perpetually aged and yet always young: he has wisdom and no history. "Pay no attention to that," you will say. "We have only to welcome him without reserve; our history will be his history, or at least his son's." But that is what we take care not to do. Thus he floats on, uncertain, uprooted.

Moreover, let him not turn back toward Israel to find a community and a past to compensate for those which are refused him. That Jewish community which is based neither on nation, land, religion—at least not in contemporary France—nor material interest, but only on an identity of situation, might indeed be a true *spiritual* bond of affection, of culture, and of mutual aid. But the Jew's enemies will immediately say that this bond is ethnic, and he himself, at a loss how to designate it, will perhaps use the word *race*. Then at one stroke he has justified the anti-Semite: "You see very well that there is a Jewish *race*; they recognize it themselves, and besides they crowd together everywhere." And, in fact, if the Jews want to draw a legitimate pride from this community, they must indeed end up by exalting racial qualities, since they cannot take pride in any collective work that is specifically Jewish, or in a civilization properly Jewish, or in a common mysticism.

Thus the anti-Semite wins on all counts. In a word, the Jew, an intruder into French society, is compelled to remain isolated. If he does not consent, he is insulted. But if he consents, he is no more readily assimilated on that account; he is tolerated—and always with a distrust that drives him on each occasion to "prove himself."

In case of war or civil disturbance, the "true" Frenchman has no proofs to make; he simply fulfils his military or civil obligations. But it is not the same for the Jew. He may be sure that people are going to make a strict count of the number of Jews in the army. Thus he suddenly finds himself answerable for all his coreligionists. Even if he has passed the military age, he is going to feel the necessity of enlisting—whether he does anything about it or not—because people are pretending everywhere that Jews are slackers. A rumor not without foundation, some may say. Not at all. In an analysis of a Jewish complex made by Stekel, of which I will have more to say later, I read this passage: "The Christians said"—it was an Austrian Jewess speaking —"that the Jews always try to get out from under as much as they can. Then my husband wanted to volunteer." Now this referred to the beginning of the war of 1914, and Austria had had no war since that of 1866, which was carried on with a professional army. This slander upon the Austrian Jews, which has been spread in France also, is simply the spontaneous fruit of distrust of the Jew.

In 1938, at the time of the international crisis that was resolved at Munich, the French government called up only certain categories of the reserve. The majority of the men able to bear arms were not yet mobilized. Already, however, stones were being thrown through the store windows of one of my friends, a Jewish merchant at Belleville, on the grounds that he was a slacker. Thus the Jew, if he is to be left in peace, should be mobilized ahead of other people; in case of famine, he should be hungrier than others; if a general disaster strikes the country, he should be the one whom it hits hardest.

This perpetual obligation to prove that he is French puts the Jew in a situation of guilt. If on every occasion he does not do more than everybody else, much more than anybody else, he is guilty, he is a dirty Jew—and one might say, parodying the words of Beaumarchais: To judge by the qualities we demand of a Jew if he is to be assimilated as a "true" Frenchman, how many Frenchmen would be found worthy of being Jews in their own country?

Since the Jew is dependent upon opinion for his profession, his rights, and his life, his situation is completely unstable. Legally not open to attack, he is at the mercy of the whims and passions of the "real" society. He carefully watches the progress of anti-Semitism; he tries to foresee crises and gauge trends in the same way that the peasant keeps watch on the weather and predicts storms. He ceaselessly calculates the effects that external events will have on his own position. He may accumulate legal guarantees, riches, honors; he is only the more vulnerable on that account, and he knows it. Thus it seems to him at one and the same time that his efforts are always crowned with success—for he knows the astonishing successes of his race—and that a curse has made them empty, for he will never acquire the security enjoyed by the most humble Christian.

This is perhaps one of the meanings of *The Trial* by the Jew, Kafka. Like the hero of that novel, the Jew is engaged in a long trial. He does not know his judges, scarcely even his lawyers; he does not know what he is charged with, yet he knows that he is considered guilty; judgment is continually put off—for a week, two weeks—he takes advantage of these delays to improve his position in a thousand ways, but every precaution taken at random pushes him a little deeper into guilt. His external situation may appear brilliant, but the interminable trial invisibly wastes him away, and it happens sometimes, as in the novel, that men seize him, carry him off on the pretense that he has lost his case, and murder him in some vague area of the suburbs.

The anti-Semites are right in saying that the Jew eats, drinks, reads, sleeps, and dies like a Jew. What else could he do? They have subtly poisoned his food, his sleep, and even his death. How else could it be for him, subjected every moment to this poisoning? As soon as he steps outside, as soon as he encounters others, in the street or in public places, as soon as he feels upon him the look of those whom a Jewish newspaper calls "Them"—a look that is a mixture of fear, disdain, reproach, and brotherly love—he must decide: does he or does he not consent to be the person whose role they make him play? And if he consents, to what extent? If he refuses, will he refuse all kinship with other Israelites, or only an ethnic relationship?

Whatever he does, his course has been set for him. He can choose to be courageous or cowardly, sad or gay; he can choose to kill Christians or to love them; but he cannot choose not to be a Jew. Or, rather, if he does so choose, if he declares that Jews do not exist, if he denies with violence and desperation the Jewish character in himself, it is precisely in this that he is a Jew. I who am not a Jew, I have nothing to deny, nothing to prove; but if the Jew has decided that his race does not exist, it is up to him to prove it. To be a Jew is to be thrown into—to be *abandoned to*—the situation of a Jew; and at the same time it is to be responsible in and through one's own person for the destiny and the very nature of the Jewish people. For, whatever the Jew says or does, and whether he have a clear or vague conception of his responsibilities, it is as if all his acts were subject to a Kantian imperative, as if he had to ask himself before each act: "If all Jews acted as I am going to do, what would happen to Jewish life?" And to the questions he asks himself (what would happen if all the Jews were Zionists, or if, on the contrary, they were all converted to Christianity? If all Jews denied they were Jews? etc.), he must make reply, alone and unaided, by choosing himself.

If it is agreed that man may be defined as a being having freedom within the limits of a situation, then it is easy to see that the exercise of this freedom may be considered as *authentic* or *inauthentic* according to the choices made in the situation. Authenticity, it is almost needless to say, consists in having a true and lucid consciousness of the situation, in assuming the responsibilities and risks that it involves, in accepting it in pride or humiliation, sometimes in horror and hate.

There is no doubt that authenticity demands much courage and more than courage. Thus it is not surprising that one finds it so rarely. Most members of the middle class and most Christians are not authentic, in the sense that they refuse to live up to their middle-class or Christian condition fully and that they always conceal certain parts of themselves from themselves. When the Communists set down as part of their program "the radicalization of the masses," when Marx explains that the proletarian class *ought to be* conscious of itself, what does that mean if not that the worker, too, is not at first authentic?

And the Jew does not escape this rule: authenticity for him is to live to the full his condition as Jew; inauthenticity is to deny it or to attempt to escape from it. Inauthenticity is no doubt more tempting for him than for other men, because the situation which he has to lay claim to and to live in is quite simply that of a martyr. What the least favored of men ordinarily discover in their situation is a bond of concrete solidarity with other men. The economic condition of the salaried man living in the perspective of revolution, or the condition of the member of a persecuted church, involves in itself a profound unity of material and spiritual interests. But we have shown that the Jews have neither community of interests nor community of beliefs. They do not have the same fatherland; they have no history. The sole tie that binds them is the hostility and disdain of the societies which surround them. Thus the authentic Jew is the one who asserts his claim in the face of the disdain shown toward him.

The situation he wishes fully to understand and live out is, in time of social peace, almost incomprehensible: it is an atmosphere, a subtle sense of faces and of words, a menace that is concealed in things, an abstract bond that unites him to men who in all other respects

91

are very different from him. Everything conspires actually to show him to his own eyes as a simple Frenchman. For the prosperity of his affairs depends closely upon that of his country, the fate of his sons is linked to peace, to the greatness of France, and the language he speaks and the culture that has been given him permit him to base his calculations and his reasoning on the principles common to the whole nation. He should therefore only have to let himself go in order to forget that he is a Jew, if he did not detect everywhere this almost undetectable poison—the hostile consciousness of others.

What is astonishing is certainly not that there are inauthentic Jews; it is rather that, in proportion, they are fewer than the inauthentic Christians. However, it is by taking advantage of certain aspects of the conduct of inauthentic Jews that the anti-Semite has forged his general mythology of the Jew. What characterizes the inauthentic Jews is that they deal with their situation by running away from it; they have chosen to deny it, or to deny their responsibilities, or to deny their isolation, which appears intolerable to them. That does not necessarily mean that they wish to destroy the concept of the Jew or that they explicitly deny the existence of a Jewish reality. But their gestures, sentiments and acts aim secretly at destroying this reality.

In a word, the inauthentic Jews are men whom other men take for Jews and who have decided to run away from this insupportable situation. The result is that they display various types of behavior not all of which are present at the same time in the same person but each of which may be characterized as an *avenue of flight*. The anti-Semite by collecting and assembling all these distinct and often incompatible avenues of flight has traced out a monstrous portrait which is supposed to be that of the Jew in general; at the same time he explains these free efforts at escape from a painful situation as hereditary traits, engraved on the very body of Israel and, consequently, incapable of modification.

If we wish to see the problem clearly, we must take this portrait apart, restore the autonomy of these "avenues of flight," and present them in their true character as ventures in behavior instead of innate qualities. It must be understood that the description of these avenues of flight is applied solely to the *inauthentic* Jew (the term "inauthentic" implying no moral blame, of course), and that it should be supplemented by a description of authentic Jewishness. Finally, we must grasp the idea that it is the *situation* of the Jew which must under all circumstances serve us as guiding thread. If we understand this method and if we apply

93

it rigorously, perhaps we will be able to substitute for the great Manichaean myth about Israel a few truths which, while more fragmentary, are more accurate.

What is the first trait in the anti-Semitic mythology? It is, we are told, that the Jew is a complicated being who passes his time in self-analysis and subtle scheming. We are quick to call him a "splitter of hairs" without even asking ourselves whether this tendency to analysis and introspection is compatible with the sharpness in business and the blind aggressiveness that are also attributed to him. For my part, I recognize that the effort to escape produces in some Jews—for the most part intellectuals—an almost continuously reflective attitude. But again we must understand each other. This reflective behavior is not inherited. It is an avenue of flight, and it is we who force the Jew to flee.

Stekel, along with several other psychoanalysts, speaks of a "Jewish complex," and many are the Jews who mention their "inferiority complex." I see no harm in using this expression if we understand that this complex has not been received from the outside and that the Jew *creates this complex* when he chooses to live out his situation in an inauthentic manner. He has allowed himself to be persuaded by the anti-Semites; he is the first victim of their propaganda. He admits with them that, *if there is a Jew*, he must have the characteristics with which popular malevolence endows him, and his effort is to constitute himself a martyr, in the proper sense of the term, that is, to prove *in his person* that there are no Jews.

With him anxiety often takes a special form; it becomes a fear of acting or feeling like a Jew. We are familiar with those neurasthenics who are haunted by the fear of killing, of jumping out of a window, of uttering obscene words. Certain Jews are in some degree comparable to these people, though their anxiety rarely attains a pathological level. They have allowed themselves to be poisoned by the stereotype that others have of them, and they live in fear that their acts will correspond to this stereotype. Repeating a term used earlier, we may say that their conduct is perpetually overdetermined from the inside. Their acts have not only the motives which can be assigned to those of non-Jews —interest, passion, altruism, etc.—but they seek also to distinguish themselves radically from the acts catalogued as "Jewish." How many Jews are deliberately generous, disinterested, and even magnificent simply *because* the Jew is ordinarily taken to be a man of money? That in no way signifies that they have to struggle against "tendencies" to avarice—there is no reason, a priori, for Jews to be more avaricious than Christians —it means rather that their gestures of generosity are

95

poisoned by the decision to be generous. Spontaneity and deliberate choice are here inextricably mixed. The end pursued is to obtain a certain result in the external world and at the same time to prove to oneself, to prove to others, that there is no such thing as Jewish nature.

Thus many inauthentic Jews play at not being Jews. Several Jews have reported to me their curious reaction after the armistice. We know that the role of the Jews in the Resistance was admirable; it was they who formed the principal cadres before the Communists went into action; for four years they gave proof of a courage and a spirit of decision which it is a pleasure to acknowledge. However, certain of them hesitated a great deal before "resisting," for the Resistance appeared to them so completely in line with Jewish interests that they were reluctant at first to engage in it; they wanted to make sure they were resisting not *as Jews* but *as Frenchmen.* This scrupulousness shows sufficiently the peculiar quality of their deliberations: the Jewish factor intervenes on every occasion and it is impossible for them to make a decision based merely on the pure and simple examination of the facts. In a word, they fall naturally into a state of reflective self-consciousness.

Like the timid person, like the scrupulous person, the Jew is not content to act or think; he sees himself act, he sees himself think. We must remark, however, that Jewish reflectiveness is in itself *practical*, since it does not originate in disinterested curiosity or in the desire for moral conversion. It is not the man but the *Jew* whom the Jews seek to know in themselves through introspection; and they wish to know him *in order to deny him*. With them it is not a question of recognizing certain faults and combating them, but of underlining by their conduct the fact that they do not have those faults. Thus we may explain that particular quality of Jewish irony which exercises itself most often at the expense of the Jew himself and which is a perpetual attempt to see himself from the outside. The Jew, because he knows he is under observation, takes the initiative and attempts to look at himself through the eyes of others. This objectivity toward himself is still another ruse of inauthenticity: while he contemplates himself with the "detachment" of another, he feels himself in effect *detached* from himself; he becomes another person, a pure witness.

However, he knows that this detachment from himself will be effective only if it is ratified by others. That is why one finds in him so often the faculty of assimilation. He absorbs all knowledge with an avidity which is not to be confused with disinterested curiosity. He hopes to become "a man," nothing but a man, a man like all other men, by taking in all the thoughts of man and acquiring a human point of view of the universe. He cultivates himself in order to destroy the Jew in himself, as if he wished to have applied to him—but in modified form—the phrase of Terence: *Nil humani alienum puto ergo homo sum.* *

At the same time he tries to lose himself in the crowd of Christians. We have seen that the latter have the art and the audacity to pretend before the Jew that they are not *another race*, but purely and simply *men;* if the Jew is fascinated by Christians it is not because of their virtues, which he values little, but because they represent anonymity, humanity without race. If he tries to penetrate the most exclusive circles, it is not because of that boundless ambition with which he is reproached so often—or, rather, that ambition has only one meaning: the Jew seeks to be recognized as a man by other men. If he wishes to slip in everywhere, it is because he cannot be at rest so long as there remains a single place which resists him and which, by resisting him, makes him a Jew in his own eyes. The principle behind this drive toward assimilation is an excellent one: the Jew is claiming his rights as a Frenchman. Unfortunately the realization of this enterprise rests on an inadequate foundation. He wants people to receive him as "a man,"

---

* "Nothing human is alien to me; therefore, I am a man."

but even in the circles which he has been able to enter, he is received as a Jew. He is the rich or powerful Jew whom it is absolutely necessary to associate with, or the "good" Jew, the exceptional Jew, with whom one associates *in spite of* his race.

The Jew is not unaware of this, but if he admitted to himself that he was received as a Jew his enterprise would lose all meaning and he would become discouraged. He is therefore acting in bad faith: he is concealing the truth from himself, though he knows it in his heart. He conquers a position in his capacity as Jew; he keeps it with the means he has at his disposal, that is, with "Jewish" means, but he considers that each new conquest is a symbol of a higher step in the process of assimilation. It develops automatically that anti-Semitism, which is the almost immediate reaction of the circles he has penetrated, does not long permit him to remain unaware of what he would so much like to ignore. Yet the violence of the anti-Semite has the paradoxical effect of pushing the Jews to the conquest of other milieux and other groups. In short, his ambition is fundamentally a search for security, just as his snobbism —when he is a snob—is an effort to assimilate national values (pictures, books, etc.).

Thus he moves rapidly and brilliantly up through all social levels, but he remains like a hard kernel in the circles which accept him, and his assimilation is as ephemeral as it is brilliant. He is often reproached for this. According to a remark by André Siegfried, the Americans believe that their anti-Semitism originates in the fact that Jewish immigrants, in appearance the first to be assimilated, are still Jews in the second and third generations. This is naturally interpreted as meaning that the Jew does not sincerely desire to be assimilated and that, behind a feigned adaptability, there is concealed a deliberate and conscious attachment to the traditions of his race. The truth is exactly the contrary: it is because he is never accepted as *a* man, but always and everywhere as *the* Jew that the Jew is unassimilable.

From this situation there results a new paradox: that the inauthentic Jew wants to lose himself in the Christian world and yet he remains fixed in Jewish milieux. Wherever he introduces himself in order to get away from Jewish reality, he senses that he has been accepted as a Jew and is at every moment regarded as a Jew. His life among Christians does not bring him the anonymity he seeks; rather, it is a perpetual tension. In his flight toward mankind he takes with him everywhere the image which haunts him. That is what establishes among all Jews a solidarity which is not one of action or interest, but of situation. What unites them, even more

than the sufferings of two thousand years, is the present
hostility of Christians. Insist as they may that chance
alone has grouped them in the same residential areas,
in the same apartment houses, in the same enterprises,
there is among them a strong and complex tie which is
worth analysis.

In effect, the Jew is to another Jew the only man with
whom he can say "we." What they have in common (at
least all the inauthentic Jews) is the constant temptation to consider that they "are not like other men," their
susceptibility to the opinions of others, and their blind
and desperate decision to run away from that temptation. When, therefore, they are by themselves in the
intimacy of their apartments, by eliminating the non-
Jewish witness they eliminate Jewish reality at the same
time. No doubt those Christians who have penetrated
these interiors find their inhabitants more Jewish than
ever, but that is because they have allowed themselves
to relax—which does not mean that they abandon themselves to the enjoyment of their Jewish "nature," as
they are often accused of doing, but, on the contrary,
that they forget it. What would prove this—if that were
necessary—is that very often members of the same
family do not perceive the ethnic characteristics of
their relatives (by ethnic characteristics I mean here
the biological and hereditary facts which we have ac-

cepted as incontestable). I knew a Jewish woman whose son had to make some business trips into Nazi Germany around 1934. This son had the typical characteristics of the French Jew—a hooked nose, protruding ears, etc.—but when we expressed anxiety about what might happen to him during one of his absences, his mother replied: "Oh, I am not worried; he doesn't look like a Jew at all."

Only, by a dialectic proper to the inauthentic Jew, this recourse to interiority, this effort to constitute a Jewish immanence by which each Jew instead of being the witness of others is merged in a collective subjectivity and the Christian is eliminated as an onlooker, this and all such ruses of flight are reduced to nothing by the universal and constant presence of the non-Jew. Even in their most intimate gatherings the Jews could say of the non-Jew what St. John Perse said of the sun: "He is not named but his presence is among us." They cannot ignore the fact that their very propensity to associate together defines them as Jews in the minds of the Christians. And when they emerge in public, their solidarity with their coreligionists marks them as if with a brand. The Jew who encounters another Jew in the drawing room of a Christian is a little like a Frenchman who meets a compatriot abroad. Yet the Frenchman derives pleasure from asserting to the world that

102

he is a Frenchman, whereas the Jew, even if he were the only Israelite in a non-Jewish company, would force himself not to feel that he was a Jew. When there is another Jew with him, he feels himself endangered before the others, and he who a moment before could not even see the ethnic characteristics of his son or his nephew now looks at his coreligionist with the eyes of an anti-Semite, spying out with a mixture of fear and fatalism the objective signs of their common origin.

He is so afraid of the discoveries the Christians are going to make that he hastens to give them warning, he becomes himself an anti-Semite by impatience and for the sake of the others. Each Jewish trait he detects is like a dagger thrust, for it seems to him that he finds it in himself, but out of reach, objective, incurable, and published to the world. It does not greatly matter who *manifests* the Jewish race. The moment it is manifested, all the efforts of the Jew to deny it are in vain.

We know that the enemies of Israel are ready to support their own opinion with the statement that "there is no one more anti-Semitic than the Jew." In actual fact, this anti-Semitism of the Jew is borrowed. It is first of all the painful obsession of finding in his parents, in those near him, the defects which he wishes to reject with all his strength. Stekel, in the case mentioned earlier, reports the following: "In the household and in the education of the children everything must be under the direction [of the Jewish husband]. It is even worse in society. He pursues [the wife] with his eyes and criticizes her to such a degree that she loses countenance. As a young girl, she was proud; everybody admired her distinguished and assured manner. Now she trembles all the time for fear of making a mistake; she fears the criticism that she reads in the eyes of her husband. . . . *At the least mishap, he might reproach her with acting Jewish.*"

One can well imagine this drama between two persons: the husband—critical, almost pedantic, constantly reflective—reproaching his wife for being Jewish because he is frightened to death of appearing that way himself; the woman, crushed by his hostile and pitiless look, feeling that she is mired down in "Jewishness" in spite of herself, feeling, without understanding why, that her every gesture, her every phrase, is off key, and may reveal her origin to all eyes. It is hell for both of them. But we must see, too, that this anti-Semitism of the Jew is an effort to make himself an objective witness and judge, and thus escape liability for the faults ascribed to his "race."

In the same way, there are many who apply a lucid and pitiless severity even to themselves, because this severity produces a doubling of personality by which they escape a sense of guilt through becoming *judges*. The manifest presence in another of that "Jewish reality" which he refuses to admit in himself helps to create in the inauthentic Jew a mystical and prelogical feeling of his kinship with other Jews. This sentiment is on the whole a recognition of participation—the Jews "participate" in each other; the life of each is haunted by the lives of others—and this mystical communion becomes all the stronger the more the inauthentic Jew seeks to deny that he is a Jew.

I shall give but one example in support of this statement. We know that prostitutes abroad are frequently French, and it is never pleasant for a Frenchman to encounter a Frenchwoman in a brothel in Germany or in Argentina. However, the Frenchman's sense of his participation in the national reality is of quite different nature from the Jew's sense of participation in his people. France is a *nation;* the patriot can thus consider himself as belonging to a collective reality whose form is expressed by its economic, cultural, and military activity; and if certain secondary aspects are displeasing, he is able to overlook them. That is not the reaction of a Jew who meets a Jewess under similar conditions. In spite of himself, he sees in the humiliating situation of a prostitute the humiliating situation of Israel. I have heard several anecdotes on this subject, but I shall cite only one of them, which I have heard directly from the person to whom it happened. A Jew goes to a house of prostitution, chooses one of the women, and goes upstairs with her. She tells him she is a Jew. He finds himself impotent, and very soon is overcome with an intolerable sense of humiliation that expresses itself in spasms of vomiting. It is not that sexual intercourse with a Jewess is repugnant to him—after all, Jews marry each other; it is rather the sense that he is contributing personally to the humiliation of the Jewish race in the person of the prostitute and, consequently, in his own person. In the last analysis it is *he* who is prostituted, humiliated; it is he and the whole Jewish people.

Thus, no matter what he may do, the inauthentic Jew is possessed by the consciousness of being a Jew. At that very moment when he is forcing himself by his whole conduct to deny the traits ascribed to him, he feels that he can see these traits in others, and thus they return to him indirectly. He seeks and flees his coreligionists; he affirms that he is only one man among others, and like others, yet he feels himself compromised by the demeanor of the first passer-by, if that passer-by is a Jew. He makes himself an anti-Semite in order to break all his ties with the Jewish community; yet he finds that community again in the depths of his heart, for he experiences in his very flesh the humiliations that the anti-Semites impose upon other Jews. What stamps the inauthentic Jew is precisely this perpetual oscillation between pride and a sense of inferiority, between the voluntary and passionate negation of the traits of his race and the mystic and carnal participation in the Jewish reality.

This painful and ineluctable situation may lead a certain number of them to masochism, for masochism seems to offer a temporary solution, a sort of respite or repose. What obsesses the Jew is that he is responsible for himself, like all men, that he does freely what he considers it good to do, and that, nevertheless, a hostile society always sees his acts stained with the Jewish character. Thus it seems to him that he makes himself a Jew at the very moment he forces himself to flee the Jewish reality; that he is engaged in a struggle in which he is always vanquished and in which he becomes his own enemy; and to the degree that he is conscious of being responsible for himself, it seems to him that he has the crushing responsibility of making himself a Jew before other Jews and before Christians. Through him, in spite of him, the Jewish reality exists.

Now, masochism is the desire to have oneself treated as an object. Humiliated, despised, or simply neglected, the masochist has the joy of seeing himself moved, han-

107

dled, utilized like a thing. He tries to think of himself as an inanimate thing, and thereby to abdicate his responsibilities. This complete abdication attracts certain Jews, weary of the struggle against their impalpable Jewishness, always disowned and tormented yet always renascent. They fail to see that authenticity manifests itself in revolt, and is not to be achieved merely by the admission that they are Jews; they seek only to be made Jews by the looks, the violence, the disdain of others, by having qualities and a fate *attached* to them—to be Jews as a stone is a stone: thus for a moment they can find relief from that bewitched freedom which does not permit them to escape from their condition, and which seems to exist only in order to impose upon them a responsibility for what they reject with all their strength.

To be sure, one must recognize that this masochism has other causes as well. In an admirable and cruel passage of *Antigone*, Sophocles writes: "You have too much pride for a person sunk in misfortune." It might be said that one of the essential traits of the Jew is that, in contrast to Antigone, an everyday acquaintance with misfortune makes him modest in catastrophe. It is not to be concluded from this, as is often done, that he is arrogant when he succeeds and abject when he fails. It is quite another matter: he has assimilated the curious

108

advice which Greek wisdom gave to the daughter of Oedipus; he has learned that modesty, silence, patience are proper to misfortune, because misfortune is already a sin in the eyes of men. And certainly such wisdom can turn into masochism, into a taste for suffering. But the essential thing is still the temptation to be divested of oneself, and to be marked finally and forever with the nature and the destiny of a Jew, relieved of all responsibility and need to struggle.

Thus the anti-Semitism and the masochism of the inauthentic Jew represent in a sense the two extremes of his possible behavior: in anti-Semitism he denies his race in order to be no more than a pure individual, a man without blemish in the midst of other men; in masochism, he repudiates his liberty as a man in order to escape the sin of being a Jew and in order to seek the repose and passivity of a thing.

But the anti-Semite adds a new touch to the portrait: the Jew, he tells us, is an abstract intellectual, a pure reasoner. And we perceive at once that the terms *abstract, rationalist, intellectual* here take on a pejorative sense; it could not be otherwise, since the anti-Semite lays claim to a concrete and irrational possession of the values of the nation.

But if we recall that rationalism was one of the principal instruments of human liberation, we must refuse

109

to consider it a pure play of abstractions; on the contrary, we must insist on its creative power. In rationalism two centuries—and not the least important—placed all their hope; from rationalism sprang the sciences and their practical application; it was an ideal and a passion; it tried to bring men together by uncovering for them universal truths on which they could all reach agreement, and in its naive and agreeable optimism it deliberately confounded evil with error. We shall understand nothing about Jewish rationalism if we see it as some kind of abstract taste for disputation, instead of what it is—a youthful and lively love of men.

At the same time, however, it is also an avenue of flight—I may even say, the royal road of flight. Up to this point, we have discussed those Jews who attempt, in their individual personalities, to deny their situation as Jews. But there are others who have chosen to espouse a conception of the world that excludes the very idea of race. No doubt this is really an attempt to conceal from themselves their own situation as Jews; but if they could succeed in persuading themselves and others that the very idea of Jews is contradictory, if they could succeed in establishing their vision of the world in such fashion that they became blind to the reality of Jewishness just as the color-blind person is blind to red or green, could they not then declare in good faith that they are "men among men"?

The rationalism of Jews is a passion—the passion for the universal. If they have chosen this rather than something else, it is in order to fight the particularist conceptions that set them apart. Of all things in the world, reason is the most widely shared; it belongs to everybody and to nobody; it is the same to all. If reason exists, then there is no French truth or German truth; there is no Negro truth or Jewish truth. There is only one Truth, and he is best who wins it. In the face of universal and eternal laws, man himself is universal. There are no more Jews or Poles; there are men who live in Poland, others who are designated as "of Jewish faith" on their family papers, and agreement is always possible among them as soon as discussion bears on the universal.

Recall the portrait of the philosopher that Plato sketches in the *Phaedo:* how the awakening to reason is for him death to the body, to particularities of character; how the disembodied philosopher, pure lover of abstract and universal truth, loses all his individual traits in order to become a universal look of inquiry. It is precisely this sort of disincarnation that certain Jews seek. The best way to feel oneself no longer a Jew is to reason, for reasoning is valid for all and can be retraced by all. There is not a Jewish way of mathematics; the Jewish mathematician becomes a universal man when he reasons. And the anti-Semite who follows his reasoning becomes his brother, despite his own resistance.

Thus the rationalism to which the Jew adheres so passionately is first of all an exercise of asceticism and of purification, an escape into the universal. The young Jew who feels a taste for brilliant and abstract argument is like the infant who touches his body in order to become acquainted with it: he experiments with and inspects his intoxicating condition as universal man; on a superior level he realizes that accord and assimilation which is denied him on the social level. The choice of rationalism is for him the choice of a human destiny and a human nature. That is why it is at once both true and false that the Jew is "more intelligent than the Christian." We should say rather that he has a taste for pure intelligence, that he loves to exercise it with reference to anything and everything, that the use he makes of it is not thwarted by the innumerable taboos which still affect the Christian, or by a certain type of particularist sensibility which the non-Jew cultivates willingly. And we should add that there is in the Jew a sort of impassioned imperialism of reason: for he wishes not only to convince others that he is right; his

112

goal is to persuade them that there is an absolute and unconditioned value to rationalism. He feels himself to be a missionary of the universal; against the universalism of the Catholic religion, from which he is excluded, he asserts the "catholicity" of the rational, an instrument by which to attain to the truth and establish a spiritual bond among men. It is not by chance that Léon Brunschvicg, a Jewish philosopher, brings together in his writings the progress of reason and the progress of *unification* (unification of ideas, unification of men).

The anti-Semite reproaches the Jew with "not being creative," with having "a destructive intelligence." This absurd accusation (Spinoza, Proust, Kafka, Darius Milhaud, Chagall, Einstein, Bergson—are they not Jews?) has been given a semblance of truth by the fact that the Jewish intelligence willingly takes a critical turn. But here again it is not a question of the disposition of cerebral cells but of a choice of weapons. In effect, the Jew finds arrayed against him the irrational powers of tradition, of race, of national destiny, of instinct: it is pretended that these powers have built monuments, a culture, a history—practical values that retain much of the irrationality of their origins and are accessible only to intuition. The defense of the Israelite is to deny intuition as well as the irrational, to make the

113

obscure powers vanish—magic, unreason, everything that cannot be explained on the basis of universal principles, everything that betrays a tendency to the singular and the exceptional. He is distrustful on principle of those totalities which the Christian mind from time to time produces: he *challenges*.

No doubt in this connection one can speak of destruction, but what the Jew wishes to destroy is strictly localized; it is the ensemble of irrational values that present themselves to immediate cognition without proof. The Jew demands proof for everything that his adversary advances, because thus he proves himself. He distrusts intuition because *it is not open to discussion* and because, in consequence, it ends by separating men. If he reasons and disputes with his adversary, it is to establish the unity of intelligence. Before any debate he wishes agreement on the principles with which the disputants start; by means of this preliminary agreement he offers to construct a human order based on the universality of human nature. The perpetual criticism with which he is reproached conceals a naive love for a communion in reason with his adversaries, and the still more naive belief that violence is in no way necessary in human relations. Where the anti-Semite, the fascist, etc., starting out with intuitions that are incommunicable and that he wishes to be incommunicable, must use force in order to impose the illuminations he cannot impart, the inauthentic Jew seeks to dissolve by critical analysis all that may separate men and lead them to violence, since it is he who will be the first victim of that violence.

I am aware that Spinoza, Husserl, and Bergson have made place for intuition in their systems. But the intuition of Spinoza and Husserl is *rational,* which means that it is based on reason, is guaranteed by criticism, and has universal truth as its object. It has no resemblance to the Pascalian subtlety of spirit, and it is this latter—unanswerable, emotional, based on a thousand imperceptible perceptions—which to the Jew seems his worst enemy. As for Bergson, his philosophy offers the curious appearance of an anti-intellectualist doctrine constructed entirely by the most rational and most critical of intelligences. It is through argument that he establishes the existence of pure duration, of philosophic intuition; and that very intuition which discovers duration or life, is itself universal, since anyone may practice it, and it leads toward the universal, since its objects can be named and conceived. I realize that Bergson has his hesitations about using language, but in the end he permits words to serve as guides, as indicators, as half-faithful messengers. Who would ask more of them? And notice how completely at ease he is

115

in argument. Read again the first chapter of the essay on immediate sense data, the classical criticism of psycho-physiological parallelism, the criticism of Broca's theory of aphasia.

In fact, just as it was possible to say with Poincare that non-Euclidean geometry is a matter of definition and comes into being as soon as it is decided to call a certain type of curve straight—for example, the circumferences that may be traced on the surface of a sphere—so the philosophy of Bergson is a rationalism which exercises the privilege of a special language. Bergson has chosen, in effect, to apply the terms "life," "pure duration," etc., to what earlier philosophers had called "matter," and the comprehension of this matter he has called "intuition." Since that comprehension must be prepared for by research and criticism, since it takes hold of a universal and not of incommunicable particularities, it amounts to the same thing whether we call it irrational intuition or a synthetic function of reason. If—quite properly—we characterize the philosophy of Kierkegaard or of Novalis as irrationalism, then perhaps Bergson's system is a rationalism that has undergone a change of name.

For my part, I see it as the supreme defense of the persecuted: to attack in order to defend oneself, to conquer the irrationalism of the adversary on its own ground—that is, to render it harmless and assimilate it to constructive reason. And, as a matter of fact, where the irrationalism of a Sorel leads straight to violence, and, in consequence, to anti-Semitism, the irrationalism of Bergson is perfectly harmless and can serve only a universal reconciliation.

This universalism, this critical rationalism, is what one normally finds in the democrat. In his abstract liberalism, he affirms that Jews, Chinese, Negroes ought to have the same rights as other members of society, but he demands these rights for them as men, not as concrete and individual products of history. Thus certain Jews look at their own personalities with the eyes of the democrat. Haunted by the specter of violence, by the unassimilated residues of particularist and warrior societies, they dream of a contractual community in which thought itself would be established under form of contract—since it would be a dialogue in which the disputants would agree on principles at the start—and in which the "social contract" would be the sole collective bond. The Jews are the mildest of men, passionately hostile to violence. That obstinate sweetness which they conserve in the midst of the most atrocious persecution, that sense of justice and of reason which they put up as their sole defense against a hostile, brutal, and unjust society, is perhaps the best part of the mes-

117

sage they bring to us and the true mark of their greatness.

But the anti-Semite at once seizes on this free effort of the Jew to live in and master his situation; he makes it into a fixed characteristic manifesting the Jew's incapacity to become assimilated. For him, the Jew is no longer a rationalist but a reasoner; his quest is not a positive search for the universal, but proof of his incapacity to take hold of vital racial and national values; the spirit of free criticism on which he bases his hope of defending himself against superstition and myth becomes the satanic spirit of negation, a virus of destruction. Instead of appreciating this spirit as an instrument of self-criticism originating spontaneously in modern society, the anti-Semite sees it as a permanent threat to national ties and French values.

Rather than deny the love of certain Jews for the exercise of reason, it has seemed to me more true and more useful to attempt to explain it.

It is also as an attempt to escape that we must interpret the attitude some Jews assume toward their own bodies.

We know that the sole ethnic characteristics of the Jews are physical. The anti-Semite has seized upon this fact and has transformed it into a myth: he pretends to be able to detect his enemy at one glance. The reaction of certain Israelites, therefore, is to deny the body that betrays them. Naturally this negation will vary in intensity as their physical appearance is more or less revealing; in any case, they do not feel toward their bodies that complacency, that tranquil sentiment of property which characterizes most "Aryans."

For these latter the body is a fruit of the French soil; they possess it by that same profound and magical participation which assures them the enjoyment of their land and their culture. Because they are proud of it, they have attached to it a certain number of values that are strictly irrational but are intended to express the idea of *life* as such. Scheler has accurately called them "vital values"; in effect, they concern neither the elementary needs of the body nor the demands of the spirit, but a certain blossoming, a certain biological style that seems to be a manifestation of the intimate functioning of the organism, the harmony and independence of the organs, the cellular metabolism, and above all the "life plan," that blind and wily design which is the very essence of life. Grace, nobility, vivacity are among these values. In fact, we ascribe them even to animals: we speak of the grace of a cat, of the nobility of the eagle.

It is obvious that people introduce a great number of these biological values into the concept of *race*. Is not race itself a pure vital value; does it not enclose in its basic structure a judgment of value, since the very idea of race implies that of inequality? Hence the Christian, the Aryan, feels his body in a special way. He does not have a pure and simple consciousness of the massive modifications of his organs; the messages and appeals that his body sends him come with certain coefficients of ideality, and are always more or less symbolic of vital values. He even devotes a portion of his activity to procuring perceptions of himself that correspond to his vital ideal: the nonchalance of the elegant, the vivacity and "stir" which characterize the stylish manner in certain epochs, the ferocious air of the Italian fascist, the grace of women—all these seek to express the aristocracy of the body. And to these values are naturally linked some anti-values, such as the discredit attaching to the "lower functions" of the body, or certain codes of behavior and sentiments—modesty, for example. The latter, certainly, is not merely a sense of shame at showing one's nakedness; it is also a way of making the body precious, a refusal to see the body as a mere instrument: the body is hidden in its sanctuary of clothing like an object of adoration.

The inauthentic Jew is deprived of his vital values by the Christian. If he becomes conscious of his body, the concept of race immediately appears to poison his in-

120

timate sensations. The values of nobility and grace have been pre-empted by the Aryans, who refuse them to him. If he accepted these values he would be constrained perhaps to reconsider the notion of ethnic superiority with all its consequences. In the very name of *universal man,* he refuses to lend an ear to the private messages his organism sends him; in the name of *rationality* he rejects irrational values and accepts only spiritual values. Universality being for him at the summit of the scale of values, he conceives of a sort of *universal and rationalized body.* He does not have an ascetic's disdain for his body, he does not call it a "rag" or a "beast," but neither does he see it as an object of veneration. Insofar as he does not actually forget it, he treats it as an instrument, which he concerns himself with only in order to adapt it with precision to his ends.

And just as he refuses to consider the irrational values of life, so he refuses to set up a hierarchy among the natural functions. This refusal has two purposes: on the one hand it entails a denial of the ethnic specificity of Israel, and on the other it is an offensive weapon aimed at persuading Christians that their bodies are only instruments. That "lack of shame" with which the anti-Semite reproaches certain Jews has no other origin. It is primarily an effort to treat the body rationally. If the body is a mechanism, why cast an interdict upon its needs of excretion? Why exercise a perpetual control over it? It must be cared for, cleaned, maintained, without joy, without love, and without shame—like a machine.

And sometimes, indeed, there is also a certain despair behind this lack of shame: what is the good of veiling a body that the gaze of the Aryans has denuded once and for all? To be a Jew in the eyes of the world—is that not worse than being naked? Of course, this rationalism is not confined to the Jews: there are a good many Christians—doctors, for example—who assume such a rational point of view toward their own bodies, or the bodies of their children. But in such cases it is a matter of a conquest, of an enfranchisement which coexists, usually, with many prelogical survivals. The Jew, on the other hand, is not trying to criticize the vital values; he has become such that he has no feeling of them.

It should be added, however, as a point against the anti-Semite, that this bodily uneasiness that occurs among Jews may have quite opposite results and may lead to shame of the body and an extreme modesty. I have been told of many Jews who go far beyond most Christians in this respect and whose constant concern is to conceal their bodies. And there are others who are preoccupied with spiritualizing their bodies, that is, clothing them in spiritual signification, since they deny them vital values; to a Christian the faces and gestures of certain Jews are often embarrassing because of what they signify—they express intelligence, goodness, resignation, or pain too clearly and for too long a time.

It is customary to make fun of the rapid and voluble gestures that the Jew makes with his hands when he speaks—though this mimic vivacity is actually less widespread than people think. It is highly important that we distinguish this trait from behavior that resembles it in appearance, such as that of the typical citizen of Marseille, for example. The mimicry of the Marseillais—exaggerated, rapid, unquenchable—goes with his interior fire, his constant nervousness, his desire to render with the whole body what he sees and what he feels. In the Jew there is primarily a desire to be totally meaningful, to feel the organism as a medium in the service of an idea, to transcend the body that weighs him down and go beyond it toward objects or truths susceptible to reason. Let me hasten to add that in such delicate matters we must protect ourselves with all sorts of reservations. What we have just said does not apply to all inauthentic Jews; above all, it varies in importance with the general attitude of the Jew, depending on his education, his origin, and especially the general pattern of his behavior.

It seems to me that one might explain in the same way the famous Jewish "lack of tact." (Of course, there is a considerable amount of malice in this accusation.) In the last analysis what we call tact is connected with "subtlety of spirit," a thing the Jew does not trust. To act with tact is to appreciate a situation at a glance, to embrace it as a whole, to feel it rather than to analyze it, but it is at the same time to direct one's conduct by reference to a multitude of indistinct principles, of which some concern vital values and others express ceremonies and traditions of politeness that are altogether irrational. Thus to act "with tact" implies that the doer of the act has adopted a certain conception of the world, one that is traditional, ritual, and synthetic; one for which *he can give no reason*. It implies also a particular sense of psychological ensembles, it is in no sense *critical*, and we might add that it takes on its whole meaning only in a strictly defined community with common ideas, mores, and customs. The Jew has as much natural tact as anybody, if by that is understood a basic comprehension of others, but he doesn't *seek* to have it.

To agree to base his conduct on tact would be to recognize that reason is not a sufficient guide in human relations and that traditional and obscure powers of intuition may be superior to it when it is a question of adapting oneself to other people or of handling them. That would mean to admit a kind of casuistry, a morality of particular cases, and thus to renounce the idea of a universal human nature that demands universal treatment; it would be an admission that concrete situations, as well as concrete men, cannot be compared; it would mean a relapse into particularism. And by that the Jew would assist in his own downfall, for in the name of this tact the anti-Semite denounces him as a particular case and excludes him from the national community.

The Jew has a marked inclination to believe that the worst difficulties may be resolved by reason; he does not *see* the irrational, the magical, the concrete and particular nuance; he *does not believe* in singularities of sentiment. By a very understandable defense reaction, this man who lives by the opinion that others have of him tries to deny the values of opinion. He is tempted to apply to men the reasoning which is suited to objects; he moves toward the analytic rationalism of the engineer and the worker: not because he is formed or attracted by objects but because he is rejected by men. And the analytical psychology he constructs permits him readily to reduce the synthetic structures of consciousness to a play of interests, to the composition of appetites, to the algebraic sum of tendencies. The art of dominating, of reducing, or of persuading becomes a rational calculation. Only, it follows inevitably that this explanation of human conduct by universal notions entails the risk of abstraction.

Indeed, it is the taste for abstraction that explains the Jew's special relationship to money. Jews love money, we are told. Yet this collective consciousness that is eager to paint the Jew as avid for gain rarely confuses him with that other popular myth of the miser: the munificent prodigality of the Jew is even a favorite theme of the anti-Semite's accusations. Certainly, if the Jew loves money, it is not because he has any particular appetite for copper or gold or bank notes: for him money often assumes the abstract form of shares of stock, checks, bank deposits—it is not to its sensible configuration but to its abstract form that he becomes attached.

Actually it is the power of purchase that appeals to him, and if he prefers this form of property to all others it is because it is universal. Appropriation by purchase does not depend on the race of the buyer; it does not vary with his idiosyncrasies. The *price* of the object is set in reference to *any* buyer, who is set apart only by the fact that he has the amount written on the ticket. And when that sum is paid, the buyer is legally proprietor of the object. Thus property by purchase is an

126

abstract and universal form of proprietorship, in contrast to the singular and irrational ownership by participation.

Here there is a vicious circle: The richer a Jew is, the greater the tendency of the traditionalist anti-Semite to insist that true property is not legal property but an adaptation of body and spirit to the object possessed. In this way, as we have seen, the poor man recovers the soil and the spiritual goods of France. Anti-Semitic literature abounds in proud replies addressed to Jews by virtuous orphans and ruined old nobles, the substance of which is that honor, love, virtue, taste, etc., are "not to be bought." But the more the anti-Semite insists on this sort of possession—which aims to exclude the Jews from the community—the more the Jew will be tempted to affirm that the sole form of property is legal property gained through purchase. In opposition to that magical possession that is refused him and which deprives him even of the objects he has bought, he becomes attached to money as the legitimate power of appropriation by the universal and anonymous man he seeks to be. If he insists on the power of money, it is to defend his rights as a consumer in a community that contests them, and it is at the same time to rationalize the bond of possessor to object possessed in order to bring property into the framework of a ra-

127

tional conception of the universe. In effect, purchase, as a rational commercial act, legitimizes property, which becomes in these terms simply a right of use. At the same time, the *value* of the object, instead of appearing as some mystic mana accessible only to the initiate, becomes identified with its price, which is published and can be immediately known by anybody.

Thus we see all the background for the Jew's alleged taste for money. If money defines value, then value is universal and rational; it does not emanate from obscure social sources, it is accessible to all. The Jew cannot then be excluded from society: he becomes a part of it as anonymous purchaser and as consumer. Money is a factor of integration. To the fine formulas of the anti-Semite—"Money can't do everything"—"There are things money can't buy"—the Jew replies sometimes by affirming the absolute power of money: "Anybody can be bought, if you can just find his price." This is not cynicism or baseness; it is merely a counterattack. The Jew would like to persuade the anti-Semite that irrational values are a pure appearance and that there is no one who is not ready to turn them in for cash. And if the anti-Semite lets himself be bought, there is the proof—proof that at heart he also prefers legal appropriation by purchase to mystical appropriation by participation. At one stroke the Jew becomes anonymous; he is no more than a universal man who is defined solely by his power to buy. Thus are explained at one and the same time the Jew's "eagerness for gain" and his very real generosity. His "love of money" merely indicates his deliberate decision to consider valid only the rational, universal, and abstract ties that men have with things; the Jew is a utilitarian because opinion refuses him all enjoyment of things except *use*. At the same time he wishes to acquire through money the social rights that are refused him as an individual. He is not shocked at being loved for his money; the respect and adulation riches procure for him go to the anonymous being who possesses such a power of purchase. It is precisely this anonymity he seeks, for, paradoxically, he wishes to be rich in order to escape notice.

These comments should permit us to see the principal traits of Jewish sensibility. It is, one suspects, deeply marked by the choice the Jew makes of himself and how he understands his situation. But we do not intend to draw a portrait here. We shall only recall the long patience of the Jew and his expectation of persecution, that presentiment of catastrophe which he seeks to hide from himself during happy years but which bursts out suddenly in prophetic vision as soon as the skies darken. We shall emphasize the particular form of his humanism, that will to universal brotherhood which collides with the most obstinate of particularisms, and the bizarre mixture of love, hate, admiration, and distrust that he feels toward those men who wish to have nothing to do with him.

Do not believe that if you go up to him with your arms outspread, he will give you his confidence. He has learned to detect anti-Semitism under the most noisy protestations of liberalism. He is as distrustful of Christians as workers are of those young members of the middle class who have "a love for the people." His utilitarian psychology leads him to look for self-interest, calculation, and the pretense of tolerance behind the manifestations of sympathy that some people lavish on him. And he is rarely mistaken. Yet he seeks eagerly for these very manifestations; he loves the honors that he mistrusts; he wants to be on the other side of the social barrier—with the others, among the others; he caresses the impossible dream of being suddenly rescued from universal suspicion by real affection, by evident proofs of good will.

We must understand this world of extremes, this humanity cut in two; we must see that every Jewish sentiment has a different quality depending on whether it is addressed to a Christian or a Jew. The love of a Jew for a Jewess is not of the same nature as the love he may feel for an "Aryan" woman. There is a basic doubling

130

of Jewish sensibility concealed beneath the exterior of a universal humanism.

Finally, we should note the disarming freshness and the uncultivated spontaneity of Jewish feelings. Completely given over to rationalizing the world, the inauthentic Israelite can no doubt analyze his affections, but he cannot cultivate them: it is possible for him to be Proust, but not Barrès. This is because the culture of sensibility and of the self presupposes a profound traditionalism, a taste for the particular and the irrational, a recourse to empirical methods, the tranquil enjoyment of deserved privileges: all these the principles of an aristocratic sensibility. A Christian will derive from this the tendency to treat himself like a luxurious plant, or like those barrels of good wine that are sent to the Indies only to be brought back at once to France, so that the sea air may penetrate them and give the wine an unparalleled savor. The culture of the ego is entirely magical and participationist, yet the continual turning of attention toward oneself does in the end bear some fruit. The Jew who is fleeing from his self and who conceives of psychological processes as mechanical functionings rather than as the flowering of an organism, does no doubt observe the play of his inclinations, for he has placed himself on a reflective level, but he does not cultivate them; he is not even sure

131

that he gets their real meaning: introspective analysis is not the best instrument for psychological inquiry. Thus the rationalist is constantly overwhelmed by a fresh and powerful mass of passions and emotions. He joins crude sensibility to the refinements of intellectual culture. There is a sincerity, a youth, a warmth in the manifestations of friendship of a Jew that one will rarely find in a Christian, hardened as the latter is by tradition and ceremony. This is also what gives such a disarming character to Jewish suffering, the most over-whelming of sufferings.

But it is not necessary to labor this point. It is enough to have indicated the consequences that Jewish inau-thenticity may have.

We shall content ourselves in conclusion with indi-cating in broad strokes what is called Jewish uneasi-ness. For Jews are often uneasy. An Israelite is never sure of his position or of his possessions. He cannot even say that tomorrow he will still be in the country he inhabits today, for his situation, his power, and even his right to live may be placed in jeopardy from one moment to the next. Besides, as we have seen, he is haunted by that impalpable and humiliating image which the hostile mob has of him. His history is one of wandering over the course of twenty centuries; at any moment he must be ready to pick up his stick and his

132

bundle. Ill at ease even inside his own skin, the unreconciled enemy of his own body, following the impossible dream of an assimilation that constantly recedes, he can never have the security of the "Aryan," firmly established on his land and so certain of his property that he can even forget that he is a proprietor and see the bond that unites him to his country as *natural*.

However, it should not be thought that Jewish uneasiness is metaphysical. It would be an error to identify it with the anxiety that moves us to a consideration of the condition of man. I should say rather that metaphysical uneasiness is a condition that the Jew—no more than the worker—cannot allow himself today. One must be sure of one's rights and firmly rooted in the world, one must be free of the fears that each day assail oppressed minorities or classes, before one dare raise questions about the place of man in the world and his ultimate destiny. In a word, metaphysics is the special privilege of the Aryan governing classes. Let no one see in this an attempt to discredit metaphysics; when men are liberated, it will become again an essential concern of mankind.

The disquietude of the Jew is not metaphysical; it is social. The ordinary object of his concern is not yet the place of man in the universe, but his place in society. He cannot perceive the loneliness of each man in the midst of a silent universe, because he has not yet emerged from society into the world. It is among men that he feels himself lonely; the racial problem limits his horizon. Nor is his uneasiness of the kind that seeks perpetuation; he takes no pleasure in it—he seeks reassurance.

It has been called to my attention that there have been no Jewish surrealists in France. That is because surrealism, in its own way, raises the question of human destiny. Its destructive activities and the great fanfare raised over them were the luxurious games of young members of the middle class completely at ease in a victorious country that belonged to them. The Jew does not dream of destroying, or of considering the condition of man in its nudity. He is the social man *par excellence,* because his torment is social.

It is society, not the decree of God, that has made him a Jew and brought the Jewish problem into being. As he is forced to make his choices entirely within the perspective set by this problem, it is in and through the social that he chooses even his own existence. His constructive effort to integrate himself in the national community is social; social is the effort he makes to think of himself, that is, to situate himself, among other men; his joys and sorrows are social; but all this is because the curse that rests upon him is social. If in consequence he is reproached for his metaphysical inauthenticity, if attention is called to the fact that his constant uneasiness is accompanied by a radical positivism, let us not forget that these reproaches return upon those who make them: the Jew is social because the anti-Semite has made him so.

Such, then, is this haunted man, condemned to make his choice of himself on the basis of false problems and in a false situation, deprived of the metaphysical sense by the hostility of the society that surrounds him, driven to a rationalism of despair. His life is nothing but a long flight from others and from himself. He has been alienated even from his own body; his emotional life has been cut in two; he has been reduced to pursuing the impossible dream of universal brotherhood in a world that rejects him.

Whose is the fault? It is our eyes that reflect to him the unacceptable image that he wishes to dissimulate. It is our words and our gestures—*all* our words and *all* our gestures—our anti-Semitism, but equally our condescending liberalism—that have poisoned him. It is we who constrain him to choose to be a Jew whether through flight from himself or through self-assertion; it is we who force him into the dilemma of Jewish authenticity or inauthenticity. We have created this variety of men who have no meaning except as artificial

135

products of a capitalist (or feudal) society, whose only reason for existing is to serve as scapegoat for a still prelogical community—this species that bears witness for essential humanity better than any other because it was born of secondary reactions within the body of humanity—this quintessence of man, disgraced, uprooted, destined from the start to either inauthenticity or martyrdom. In this situation there is not one of us who is not totally guilty and even criminal; the Jewish blood that the Nazis shed falls on all our heads.

The fact remains, you may anwer, that the Jew is free: he can choose to be authentic. That is true, but we must understand first of all that *that does not concern us*. The prisoner is always free to try to run away, if it is clearly understood that he risks death in crawling under the barbed wire. Is his jailer any less guilty on that account?

Jewish authenticity consists in choosing oneself *as Jew*—that is, in realizing one's Jewish condition. The authentic Jew abandons the myth of the universal man; he knows himself and wills himself into history as a historic and damned creature; he ceases to run away from himself and to be ashamed of his own kind. He unde stands that society is bad; for the naive monism of the inauthentic Jew he substitutes a social pluralism. He knows that he is one who stands apart, untouchable,

136

scorned, proscribed—and it is *as such* that he asserts his being. At once he gives up his rationalistic optimism; he sees that the world is fragmented by irrational divisions, and in accepting this fragmentation —at least in what concerns him—in proclaiming himself a Jew, he makes some of these values and these divisions his. He chooses his brothers and his peers; they are the other Jews. He stakes everything on human grandeur, for he accepts the obligation to live in a situation that is defined precisely by the fact that it is unlivable; he derives his pride from his humiliation.

The moment he ceases to be passive, he takes away all power and all virulence from anti-Semitism. The inauthentic Jew flees Jewish reality, and the anti-Semite makes him a Jew in spite of himself; but the authentic Jew *makes himself a Jew*, in the face of all and against all. He accepts all, even martyrdom, and the anti-Semite, deprived of his weapons, must be content to yelp at the Jew as he goes by, and can no longer touch him. At one stroke the Jew, like any authentic man, escapes description. The common characteristics we have attributed to the inauthentic Jews emanate from their common inauthenticity. We shall encounter none of them in the authentic Jew; he is what he makes himself, that is all that can be said. In this isolation to which he has consented, he becomes again a man, a whole man, with the meta-

137

physical horizons that go with the condition of man.

But this does not mean that we can soothe our consciences by saying: "Very well, since the Jew is free, let him be authentic, and we shall have peace." The choice of authenticity is not a solution of the social aspect of the Jewish problem; it is not even an individual solution. No doubt authentic Jews are today much more numerous than one may suspect. The suffering that the Jews have undergone during the past few years has done much to open their eyes, and it seems to me even probable that there are more authentic Jews than authentic Christians. Yet the choice they have made of themselves does not smooth their way as individuals, rather the contrary.

Take the example of one "authentic" French Jew who, after fighting in 1940, directed a French propaganda review in London during the Occupation. He wrote under a pseudonym, because he wished to avoid trouble for his "Aryan" wife, who had remained in France. This is what many French émigrés did, and when they did it, it was all right. But since he was a Jew, he was refused this right: "Aha," people said, "another Yid trying to hide his origin." Again, he chose the articles he published with strict reference to their merit. If by chance the proportion of Jewish articles was considerable, the readers sneered; they wrote to him: "I see that the happy family is getting together again." On the other hand, if he refused a Jewish article, he was accused of acting like an anti-Semite. "Oh well," you may say, "let him ignore all that, since he is authentic." That is easily said, but he cannot ignore it, precisely because he is engaged in carrying on propaganda and must therefore depend on opinion. "Very well, then; it simply means that this sort of activity is closed to Jews: they'll have to give it up." There we are: you would accept authenticity if it led straight to the ghetto. And it is you who refuse to see it as a solution to the problem.

Socially, moreover, things are no better. The circumstances we have created are such that in the end division is created among the Jews. The choice of authenticity can, in fact, lead to conflicting political decisions. The Jew can choose to be authentic by asserting his place as Jew in the French community, with all that goes with it of rights and martyrdom; he may feel that for him the best way to be French is to declare himself a *French Jew*. But he may also be led by his choice of authenticity to seek the creation of a Jewish nation possessing its own soil and autonomy; he may persuade himself that Jewish authenticity demands that the Jew be sustained by a Jewish national community.

It is not impossible that these opposing choices might

be reconciled and made complementary as two aspects of Jewish reality. But for that it would be necessary that Jewish behavior should not be constantly spied upon and should not involve the constant risk of furnishing weapons for the Jew's enemies to use against him. If we had not created for the Jew his *situation* as a Jew, it would be possible for him to exercise an option between Jerusalem and France; the immense majority of French Jews would choose to remain in France, a small number would go to increase the Jewish nation in Palestine. That would not mean that the Jew who was integrated in the French national community would preserve ties with Tel Aviv; at most, Palestine might represent in his eyes a sort of ideal value, a symbol, and certainly the existence of an autonomous Jewish community would be infinitely less dangerous to the integrity of French society than, for example, the existence of an ultramontane clergy, which we tolerate with perfect equanimity.

But the temper of our time turns so legitimate a choice into a source of conflict among our Jews. In the eyes of the anti-Semite, the establishment of a Jewish nation furnishes only another proof that the Jew is out of place in the French community. Once, he was reproached for his race; now he is regarded as coming from a foreign country: he doesn't belong here, let him go to Jerusalem. Thus authenticity, when it leads to Zionism, is harmful to the Jews who wish to remain in their original fatherland, since it gives new arguments to the anti-Semite. The French Jew becomes angered at the Zionist, whose existence complicates still further an already delicate situation, and the Zionist is angered at the French Jew, whom he accuses a priori of inauthenticity.

Thus the choice of authenticity appears to be a *moral* decision, bringing certainty to the Jew on the ethical level but in no way serving as a solution on the social or political level: the situation of the Jew is such that everything he does turns against him.

4

The preceding remarks of course make no pretense at providing a solution to the Jewish problem. But perhaps they do give us a basis for stating the conditions on which a solution might be envisaged.

In effect, we have just seen that, contrary to a widespread opinion, it is not the Jewish character that provokes anti-Semitism but, rather, that it is the anti-Semite who creates the Jew. The primary phenomenon, therefore, is anti-Semitism, a regressive social force and a conception deriving from the prelogical world. With the problem thus stated, what are we to do about it? Clearly, the solution of the problem involves a definition both of the goal to be attained and of the means for its attainment. All too often people discuss means when they are still uncertain of their goal.

In short, what can we seek? Assimilation? That is a dream; the true opponent of assimilation is not the Jew but the anti-Semite, as we have already demon-

143

strated. Since his emancipation—that is, for about a century and a half—the Jew has tried to gain acceptance in a society that rejects him. It is pointless to ask him to hasten this integration, which always recedes before him; so long as there is anti-Semitism, assimilation cannot be realized.

It is true that some people advocate the employment of drastic means. There are even Jews who suggest that all Jews be forced to change their names. But this measure would be inadequate; it would be necessary to supplement it with a policy of mixed marriages and a rigorous interdiction against Jewish religious practices —in particular, circumcision. I say quite simply: these measures would be inhumane. Possibly Napoleon might have thought of such measures, but what Napoleon sought was precisely the sacrifice of the person to the community. No democracy can seek the integration of the Jews at such a cost.

Moreover, such a procedure could be advocated only by inauthentic Jews who are a prey to a crisis of anti-Semitism; it aims at nothing less than the liquidation of the Jewish race. It represents an extreme form of the tendency we have noticed in the democrat, a tendency purely and simply to suppress the Jew for the sake of *the man*. But *the man* does not exist; there are Jews, Protestants, Catholics; there are Frenchmen, Englishmen, Germans; there are whites, blacks, yellows. In short, these drastic measures of coercion would mean the annihilation of a spiritual community, founded on custom and affection, to the advantage of the national community. Most conscious Jews would refuse assimilation if it were presented to them under this aspect. Certainly they wish to integrate themselves in the nation, but *as Jews*, and who would dare to reproach them for that? We have forced them to think of themselves as Jews, we have made them conscious of their solidarity with other Jews. Should we be astonished that they now reject a policy that would destroy Israel?

It is idle to object that they form a nation within a nation. We have attempted to show that the Jewish community is neither national nor international, neither religious, nor ethnic, nor political: it is a *quasi-historical* community. What makes the Jew is his concrete situation; what unites him to other Jews is the identity of their situations. This quasi-historical body should not be considered a foreign element in society. On the contrary, it is necessary to it. If the Church tolerated its existence at a time when the Church was all-powerful, it was because it took on certain economic functions that made it indispensable. Today those functions are open to all, but that does not mean that the Jew, as a spiritual factor, makes no contribution to the peculiar nature and

145

equilibrium of the French nation. We have described objectively, perhaps severely, the traits of the inauthentic Jew. There is not one of them that is opposed to his assimilation *as such* in the national society. On the contrary, his rationalism, his critical spirit, his dream of a contractual society and of universal brotherhood, his humanism—all these qualities make him an indispensable leaven in that society.

What we propose here is a concrete liberalism. By that we mean that all persons who through their work collaborate toward the greatness of a country have the full rights of citizens of that country. What gives them this right is not the possession of a problematical and abstract "human nature," but their active participation in the life of the society. This means, then, that the Jews—and likewise the Arabs and the Negroes—from the moment that they are participants in the national enterprise, have a right in that enterprise; they are citizens. But they have these rights *as* Jews, Negroes, or Arabs—that is, as concrete persons.

In societies where women vote, they are not asked to change their sex when they enter the voting booth; the vote of a woman is worth just as much as that of a man, but it is as a woman that she votes, with her womanly intuitions and concerns, in her full character of a woman. When it is a question of the legal rights of the

146

Jew, and of the more obscure but equally indispensable rights that are not inscribed in any code, he must enjoy those rights not as a potential Christian but precisely as a French Jew. It is with his character, his customs, his tastes, his religion if he has one, his name, and his physical traits that we *must* accept him. And if that acceptance is total and sincere, the result will be, first, to make easier the Jew's choice of authenticity, and then, bit by bit, to make possible, without violence and by the very course of history, that assimilation to which some would like to drive him by force.

But the concrete liberalism we have just described is a goal; it is in danger of becoming no more than a mere ideal if we do not determine upon the means to attain it. As we have shown, it cannot be a matter of acting on the Jew. The Jewish problem is born of anti-Semitism; thus it is anti-Semitism that we must suppress in order to resolve the problem. The question therefore comes back to this: What shall we do about anti-Semitism?

Ordinary procedures, particularly propaganda and education, are by no means without importance. It is to be hoped that the child in school will receive an education that will permit him to avoid errors of passion; but the results of such education may have only an individual reference. Likewise, we should not be afraid to prohibit by basic law statements and acts that tend to bring discredit upon any category of Frenchmen. But let us have no illusions about the effectiveness of these measures: laws have never embarrassed and will never embarrass the anti-Semite, who conceives of himself as belonging to a mystical society outside the bounds of legality. We may heap up decrees and interdictions, but they will always come from the legal France, and the anti-Semite pretends that he represents the real France.

Let us recall that anti-Semitism is a conception of the Manichaean and primitive world in which hatred for the Jew arises as a great explanatory myth. We have seen that it is not a matter of an isolated opinion, but of the total choice that a man in a situation makes of himself and of the meaning of the universe. It is the expression of a certain ferocious and mystical sense of real property. If we wish to make such a choice impossible, it will not be enough to address ourselves by propaganda, education, and legal interdictions against the liberty of the anti-Semite. Since he, like all men, exists as a free agent within a situation, it is his situation that must be modified from top to bottom. In short, if we can change the perspective of choice, then the choice itself will change. Thus we do not attack freedom, but bring it about that freedom decides on other bases, and in terms of other structures.

Political action can never be directed against the freedom of citizens; its very nature forbids it to be concerned with freedom except in a negative fashion, that is, in taking care not to infringe upon it. It acts only on situations. We have demonstrated that anti-Semitism is a passionate effort to realize a national union *against* the division of society into classes. It is an attempt to suppress the fragmentation of the community into groups hostile to one another by carrying common passions to such a temperature that they cause barriers to dissolve. Yet divisions continue to exist, since their economic and social causes have not been touched; an attempt is made to lump them all together into a single one—distinctions between rich and poor, between laboring and owning classes, between legal powers and occult powers, between city-dwellers and country-dwellers, etc., etc.—they are all summed up in the distinction between Jew and non-Jew. This means that anti-Semitism is a mythical, bourgeois representation of the class struggle, and that it could not exist in a classless society. Anti-Semitism manifests the *separation* of men and their isolation in the midst of the community, the conflict of interests and the crosscurrents of passions: it can exist only in a society where a rather loose solidarity unites strongly structured pluralities; it is a phenomenon of social pluralism. In a society

149

whose members feel mutual bonds of solidarity, because they are all engaged in the same enterprise, there would be no place for it.

Finally, anti-Semitism indicates a certain mystical and participationist liaison of man with his "goods" which results from the present system of property. Again, anti-Semitism would have no existence in a society without classes and founded on collective ownership of the instruments of labor, one in which man, freed of his hallucinations inherited from an older world, would at long last throw himself wholeheartedly into *his* enterprise—which is to create the kingdom of man. Anti-Semitism would then be cut at its roots.

Thus the authentic Jew who thinks of himself as a Jew because the anti-Semite has put him in the situation of a Jew is not opposed to assimilation any more than the class-conscious worker is opposed to the liquidation of classes. On the contrary, it is an access of consciousness that will hasten the suppression of both the class struggle and racism. The authentic Jew simply renounces *for himself* an assimilation that is today impossible; he awaits the radical liquidation of anti-Semitism for his sons. The Jew of today is in full war. What is there to say except that the socialist revolution is necessary to and sufficient for the suppression of the

150

anti-Semite? It is for the Jews *also* that we shall make the revolution.

And while we wait for it? After all, it is a lazy way out to place on a future revolution the burden of liquidating the Jewish question.

Anti-Semitism is a problem that affects us all directly; we are all bound to the Jew, because anti-Semitism leads straight to National Socialism. And if we do not respect the person of the Israelite, who will respect us? If we are conscious of these dangers, if we have lived in shame because of our involuntary complicity with the anti-Semites, who have made hangmen of us all, perhaps we shall begin to understand that we must fight for the Jew, no more and no less than for ourselves.

I am told that a Jewish league against anti-Semitism has just been reconstituted. I am delighted; that proves that the sense of authenticity is developing among the Jews. But can such a league be really effective? Many Jews, and some of the best among them, hesitate to participate because of a sort of modesty: "That's biting off too much," one of them said to me recently. And he added, rather clumsily but with undoubted sincerity and modesty: "Anti-Semitism and persecution are not important."

It is easy enough to understand this repugnance. But

we who are not Jews, should we share it? Richard Wright, the Negro writer, said recently: "There is no Negro problem in the United States, there is only a White problem." In the same way, we must say that anti-Semitism is not a Jewish problem; it is *our* problem. Since we are not guilty and yet run the risk of being its victims—yes, we too—we must be very blind indeed not to see that it is our concern in the highest degree. It is not up to the Jews first of all to form a militant league against anti-Semitism; it is up to us.

It is evident that such a league will not end the problem. Yet if it spread out all over France, if it succeeded in getting official recognition from the state, if its existence brought into being in other countries similar leagues with which it could unite to form ultimately an international association, if it intervened successfully wherever injustices were called to its attention, if it acted through the press, through propaganda and education, it would attain a triple result: First, it would permit the adversaries of anti-Semitism to know their strength and to unite in an active group; second, it would rally many hesitating people, people who have no convictions on the Jewish question, for an organized group always exercises a considerable force of attraction; finally, to an adversary who is always ready to contrast the real country with the legal country, it would offer the sight of a concrete community engaged in a particular fight having nothing to do with universalist abstractions of legality. This would take away from the anti-Semite his favorite argument, which rests on the myth of the concrete. The cause of the Jews would be half won if only their friends brought to their defense a little of the passion and the perseverance their enemies use to bring them down.

In order to awaken this passion, what is needed is not to appeal to the generosity of the Aryans—with even the best of them, that virtue is in eclipse. What must be done is to point out to each one that the fate of the Jews is *his* fate. Not one Frenchman will be free so long as the Jews do not enjoy the fulness of their rights. Not one Frenchman will be secure so long as a single Jew— in France or *in the world at large*—can fear for his life.

ABOUT THE AUTHOR

JEAN-PAUL SARTRE was born in Paris in 1905. Educated at the Ecole Normale, he then taught philosophy in provincial *lycées,* and in 1938 published his first novel, *Nausea.* During the war he completed the major work that eventually established his reputation as an existential philosopher—*Being and Nothingness* (1943). After the Liberation, he founded the socialist journal *Les Temps Modernes.* He has been a prolific playwright, producing, among other works, *No Exit* (1947), *The Devil and the Good Lord* (1951), and *The Condemned of Altona* (1959). In 1960, he published his second basic philosophical work, *Critique of Dialectical Reason.* In 1964, his account of his childhood, *Words,* received worldwide acclaim. That same year he was awarded the Nobel Prize for Literature, which he refused. In 1971–1972, the first three volumes of his ambitious study of Flaubert's life and work appeared. He died in 1980.

OTHER SCHOCKEN BOOKS
OF RELATED INTEREST

WHAT IS THE USE OF JEWISH HISTORY?
by Lucy S. Dawidowicz
"Singularly animated by historical candor, these permanent essays should keep us permanently honest." —Cynthia Ozick
0-8052-1010-5

A HISTORY OF ZIONISM
by Walter Laqueur
A brilliantly crafted account of one of the most influential and controversial movements of modern times. "Historical writing of the most thoughtful and serious kind" (*Newsweek*).
0-8052-0899-2

A HISTORY OF THE JEWS
by Cecil Roth
An outstanding single-volume history, this book describes the social, religious, and cultural development of the Jewish people from biblical times to the Six-Day War.
0-8052-0009-6

ANTISEMITISM
THE LONGEST HATRED
by Robert S. Wistrich
"A smart, clear, and deeply disturbing study. His commentary causes one to hesitate before speaking easily of the Judeo-Christian heritage."

—Paul Breines, *Washington Post Book World*
0-8052-1014-8

Available at your local bookstore,
or call toll-free: 1-800-733-3000 (credit cards only).